NEW WINE
OR OLD DECEPTION?

A BIBLICAL PERSPECTIVE
OF EXPERIENCED-BASED
CHRISTIANITY

BY ROGER OAKLAND

New Wine or Old Deception?
A Biblical Perspective of Experience–Based Christianity
by Roger Oakland
Published by **The Word for Today**
P.O. Box 8000, Costa Mesa, CA 92628
Copyright © 1995 by **The Word for Today**
Printed in the United States of America
ISBN: 0–936728–62–0
Except where otherwise indicated, all Scripture quotations are taken from *The New American Standard Bible,* © 1960, 1963, 1968, 1971, 1972, 1973, 1975, 1977, by the Lockman Foundation. Used by permission.

"Now the Bereans were of more noble character than the Thessalonians, for they received the message with great eagerness and examined the Scriptures every day to see if what Paul said was true."

Acts 17:11 NIV

Note:

On December 5, 1995, John Wimber and several of his associates traveled to Toronto, Canada and expelled the Toronto Airport Vineyard from the Association of Vineyard Churches. On January 20, 1996, the Toronto Airport Vineyard was renamed the Toronto Airport Christian Fellowship. The reader should be aware of this change when reading this book, so that all references to the Toronto Airport Vineyard can be understood accordingly.

For more information, please see the Appendix on page 116.

TABLE OF CONTENTS

Acknowledgment

I would like to especially acknowledge my good friend Lorne Pritchard for inspiring and encouraging me to write this book.

The following quote was given to me by him, a statement by John Huss, who was burned at the stake July 6, 1415:

"Seek the truth, listen to the truth, learn the truth, love the truth, speak the truth, hold the truth, defend the truth until death."[1]

Lorne Pritchard has followed and lived by these words all of his life. He has encouraged me to do the same.

Roger Oakland

---

[1] Herben, Jan, *John Huss and His Followers*, 7.

Prologue

Every Bible believing Christian accepts the Bible as God's true revelation which has been given to man. They also believe that God's Holy Spirit has been given to us to guide us to the truth. The Word and the Spirit should never disagree.

When ideas, trends, doctrines or theories surface which deviate from what the Bible teaches, those who are serious about their faith should never compromise or simply "agree to disagree" for the sake of compromising the Gospel. Like the Bereans whom we read about in the book of Acts, Christians today "should search the scriptures daily to see if these things be so" (Acts 17:11 NKJV).

We are facing a situation in Christianity that has the potential to cause a major division in the body of Jesus Christ. A "new wine," some say, is being poured out all over the world, as part of a "great last–days revival." There are many who believe that this movement is from God. There are many others who strongly believe it is not, and that many people are being deceived.

Some who endorse this "new wine" spirituality are uncertain what to believe about a number of strange manifestations that are an integral part of this movement. For example, John Wimber, head of the world wide Vineyard fellowship of churches and a strong supporter of a "signs and wonders" based Christianity, has said:

> *There's nothing in Scripture that supports these kind of phenomena that I can see, and I can't think of anything throughout the church age that would. I feel no obligation to try to explain it. It's just phenomena. It's just people responding to God.*[2]

I agree with John Wimber that things are happening today in the name of Christ that have no biblical basis. However, I strongly disagree with him in that Christians do not need to express caution regarding the kinds of human responses that are being experienced. According to the Bible, Christians do have an obligation to define their experiences within the confines of biblical parameters. Otherwise, anything and everything could be of God!

It is my deep conviction that Christians should measure and evaluate spiritual experiences in light of the Word of God. If we do not rely upon God's Word as our ultimate authority, we will enter into dangerous spiritual territory. In short, when "revelation experience" supersedes the revelation given to us from God's Word, we may be seriously deceived.

---

[2]   *Charisma* (February 1995), 26.

It is for this reason that I felt compelled to write this book. I do not believe that I have all the answers, nor that I am the final authority on the subject of what Christians should or should not believe. While in the process of writing this book, I have made an effort to go to various places around the world to see and talk with numerous people who have either encountered the "anointing" of the "new wine" or are sympathetic to the concept. I am convinced that many of these people are genuine and sincere about what they believe and are seeking after "this new blessing" or "the gift" because they want more of God in their lives. However, I am also convinced that while many of them are sincere, they have been sincerely deceived.

Before writing this book, I talked with many Christians whom I deeply respect and trust, and I prayerfully considered the consequences of writing a book of this nature. With all of this in mind, it is my strong conviction that God is our authority and His Word is our standard by which we should determine truth from error.

The Bible challenges us to give reasons for what we believe and why we believe it. It is imperative that we should defend the truth by exhorting and encouraging others to do the same. We are to do this with gentleness and respect for those who disagree (1 Peter 3:15). It is my prayer that the following pages will accomplish this purpose.

Roger Oakland

Chapter I
Defending the Truth

The Bible challenges us to be diligent about knowing the truth and defending the truth. Christians should rebuke and exhort those who stray from sound doctrine, but it must always be done in love and with understanding. However, Christians often attack each other and divide over their different views and interpretations of the Scriptures. Is there a way to examine our differences and deal with them reasonably and biblically?

Dealing With Controversy

Ever since there has been a Christian church, there has been Christian controversy. The followers of Jesus Christ have always had their differences. So how do we evaluate what is truth and what is error? Are there certain parameters we can rely upon which will help evaluate when we have found the truth or discover when we have been deceived?

There are several things we should remember when dealing with the subject of biblical controversy. First of all, when there are differences, there will always be the potential for the body of Christ to divide. Although Bible believing Christians say they believe the Bible, every Christian denomination is usually confident that what they believe is far superior to what others believe.

Although we should never compromise the truth of God's Word, we need to be careful how we defend it. What are our motives? Are these motives genuine? Is there an agenda to advance our particular point of view at the expense of others? Have we taken "the full council of God" into consideration, remembering that the Bible teaches that we should "mark those who cause division."[3]

Remember that no single person or organization has a monopoly on the truth. There are no private interpretations of the Scriptures. It is also important to consider that sometimes our own interpretations or positions can be influenced by various circumstantial factors which may have effected us by giving us a distorted or unbalanced doctrinal view.

We must always be willing to consider all that the Bible teaches rather than build our doctrines on a verse or two taken out of context. Many genuine, sincere Christians who believed they were right at one time, later discovered that they had been deceived. An "experience–based" faith that is not supported by the Scriptures opens the door for all kinds of aberrant spiritual doctrines which can be catastrophic for the proclamation of the Gospel.

---

3   Romans 16:17.

The Word is Our Guide

The apostle Paul's writings, given to us by the inspiration of the Holy Spirit, provide a basis of understanding for every believer. Although his primary mission was to proclaim the Gospel, much of Paul's time and energy was spent providing guidelines to the church so that they would be more effective in proclaiming the Gospel.

It has always been Satan's desire to "bewitch" Christians and make them ineffective. Although Paul was writing to people of his day, the truths he spoke about apply to every subsequent generation. If this is true, is it not possible that false doctrines and "destructive heresies" could creep into the church today?

The Spirit and the Word Agree

Paul and other New Testament writers also warned about a time of tremendous deception that would occur in the last days, a period of time that would occur before Jesus Christ returned. Christians have been forewarned of what to expect in God's Word. And we have the Holy Spirit of God to teach us and guide us to the truth. In every case, the Word of God and the Holy Spirit of God should agree.

Defending the Truth With Truth

Today, the body of Jesus Christ is being divided. As time passes, every denomination and church will be effected in some way. A biblically–based Christianity, that once placed Christ at the center, is giving way to an experience–based Christianity that tends to focus around feelings, emotions, manifestations and an ecumenical proclamation that all Christians should "agree to disagree."

Now, as never before, we need to get back to the anchor of the Word of God which we know to be true. We should never base our doctrines upon what a mere man says is right or wrong. We should check it out according to God's Word to see if the ideas we are endorsing are extra–biblical.

Chapter II
Presenting the Truth in Love

If we are truly in the "last days" and Christians have the potential of being deceived, then what should be done? Should we retreat into our various camps, store up our weapons, and fight until a winner is declared? Or does the Bible teach that we should defend the truth with love and compassion for others? What is the biblical way to proclaim what is right, without being so "right" that we are wrong in the way that we proclaim it?

Were They Too Right?

In the book of Revelation, Jesus commended the church of Ephesus because of their zealous desire to defend the truth. They were a group of Christians who could spot a false teacher and a false prophet quickly and accurately. They showed diligence and perseverance. In short, they hated anything and everything that was false (Revelation 2:2–3).

However, Jesus also said that He held a serious offense against them for they had "lost their first love." He stated:

Remember, therefore, from where you have fallen, and repent and do the deeds you did at first, or else I am coming to you, and will remove your lampstand out of its place – unless you repent.[4]

Certainly, it is scriptural to defend the truth with endurance and zeal. Of course, we are to hold firm to the word and be steadfast and strong. The Bereans were commended for their love of the Word and the way that they searched out the Scriptures daily. But sometimes it is possible to cross over the line when we are defending the truth. According to Jesus, a Christian can be so right that they can actually be wrong.

Remember Love

This is why Jesus told the church at Ephesus that they needed to repent. They had lost their first love – their love for God and for others. In so doing, Jesus said He would remove their lampstand – their witness and their testimony, if they did not repent and mend their ways.

Before writing this book, I spent a great deal of time praying with and consulting sound men and women of God who have lived their entire Christian lives centered upon the foundational principles of the Bible. Although they warned me that there would be a price to pay for taking a stand and defending the truth against extra–biblical Christianity, each one encouraged me to do so. They also admonished me to do so with love and concern for others as my main motivating factor.

---

[4]   Revelation 2:4-5.

My greatest desire is to see unity and harmony among believers. I deeply cherish the Word of God and long to see an authentic revival where many would turn to Jesus Christ in these last important days.

The objective of writing this book is to present a sound biblical perspective that will be a warning in order to focus the attention of those whom I respect and love in the Lord back to the word of God. It is not my intention to be too harsh, take things out of context, or malign genuine believers in Christ against me. The body of Christ is full of diversity, and this diversity can be expressed in a variety of ways. However, when diversity goes beyond the parameters of the Word of God, the Bible teaches us that we should exhort the stray sheep to come home.

All of us who call Jesus Christ our Savior should do everything we can to restore broken relationships and bind ourselves together. As Jesus said:

A new commandment I give to you, that you love one another, even as I have loved you, that you also love one another. By this all men will know you are My disciples, if you have love for one another. [5]

---

[5]   John 13:34-35.

Chapter III
The Awakening?

Some claim that God is doing a "new thing." God's Holy Spirit, they say, is being poured out over all the world and we are in the midst of a mighty end times revival. Others say that people are trying to "experience" God by seeking after outward signs or manifestations that are a work of the flesh. And still others say that what is happening is an outright delusion designed by Satan, and that many are being deceived. Is it possible to analyze these views from a biblical perspective?

The Toronto Blessing?

A church in Toronto, Canada, has become the Mecca for people seeking what has been called "a blessing from God." Thousands of people from various denominations around the world have gone there to experience the "anointing." For some of the pastors and leaders who have attended the revival meetings held there, the "Toronto Blessing" has become a commodity that has been transferred to them. Now they are able to take the "anointing" that they have received and duplicate it in their own churches that are all over the world.

A Holy Spirit Bartender?

The "touch" that can be received in Toronto actually had its origins elsewhere. Although the Toronto Vineyard in Mississauga, Ontario, has become the most well–known source for this "new spiritual blessing," the original source of the "anointing" can actually be traced to the self–professed, South–African born "Holy Spirit Bartender," Rodney Howard–Browne. According to Howard–Browne, God appointed him to be a conduit for this new "anointing" that was going to be poured out upon the Earth, as part of a great revival that would take place all over the world before Jesus returned.

Howard–Browne, like many of the other leaders and promoters of this "new spiritual movement," claims he received his power to administer the anointing when God personally appeared to him. In his own words he stated:

It felt like liquid fire...like someone poured gasoline over me and set me on fire...the best way I can describe it is that it was as shocking as if I had unscrewed a light bulb from a lamp and put my finger into the socket. I knew it was of God.[6]

The August 1994 issue of *Charisma* magazine added some further insight as to how Howard–Browne became a conduit for this so–called "last days outpouring of God's Holy Spirit." According to the article, when Howard–Browne was in South Africa in the summer of

---

6   Rodney Howard-Browne, *Manifesting the Holy Ghost* (R.H.B.E.A. Publications, 1992), 16.

1979, he spent hours praying for a deeper experience with God. In the midst of his prayers, he told God: "either you come down here and touch me, or I will come up there and touch you." According to Howard–Browne, God responded to his command.

The "gift of holy laughter," which Rodney Howard–Browne has become so famous for distributing, is only one of many outward manifestations professed to be the evidence that God is pouring out a "new wave" of His Spirit as part of a world–wide, end times revival. The uncontrollable and often hysterical laughter that is being experienced, it is said, is God's way of expressing His intimate love for us during this time.

A Laughing Revival?

A number of books have been published by the enthusiasts of the "Toronto Blessing." One of these books, called *Catch The Fire: The Toronto Blessing, An Experience of Renewal and Revival,* has been written by Guy Chevreau, a former Baptist pastor, now an adjunct teacher and author associated with the Toronto Airport Vineyard. Chevreau has become an historian and an apologist for the "Toronto Blessing," citing his own conversion as he was "drawn out" of the form of Christianity he once held, to now become a strong promoter of the "Toronto Experience."[7]

John Wimber has endorsed Chevreau's book by stating:

---

7   Guy Chevreau, *Catch the Fire: the Toronto Blessing, An Experience of Renewal and Revival* (Harper Perennial Edition, 1995), 2-12.

This book is full of the enthusiasm of the newly anointed and excited people of Toronto. I'm delighted with that, and I'm sure it will be contagious with you, the reader, as it has been with them. [8]

In the first chapter of Chevreau's book, he describes how he and his wife went to a Toronto Airport Vineyard meeting at a time when his ministry was in the process of collapsing. In his own words, he stated how he felt, and what he observed:

I came, more desperate than curious, and too desperate to be critical. As a Baptist pastor, I had personally not seen anything much by the way of the Spirit's power or presence, other than some quiet tears once in a while. It was an understatement to say that I was personally unfamiliar with the kinds of physical manifestations we saw at the Airport meetings – uncontrollable laughter and inconsolable weeping; violent shaking and falling down; people waving their arms around in windmill-like motions, or vigorous judo-like chopping with their forearms. [9]

Although Guy Chevreau did not originally experience the "experience" at this first meeting, he describes how his wife Janis 'took the joy' and was down on the floor repeatedly, hysterical with laughter. John Arnott, senior pastor of the Airport Vineyard prayed that she would stay in a state of laughter for a period of forty–eight hours. [10]

---

8   Ibid., back cover.
9   Ibid., 13.
10   Ibid., 13.

Chevreau then describes the situation that took place the following day. As the Chevreau's were expecting dinner guests, he was somewhat concerned that his wife would have properly prepared for the dinner, in light of the condition that had overcome her. When he returned home from work to check on how his wife was doing, there was no food in sight. When he asked his wife where the meal was, she "fell to the floor with hysterical laughter."

It was at this point that Chevreau decided he would go out and buy fish and chips to bring home, as his wife was in no condition to cook. Then he further describes the unusual experience that followed:

> *On my return, our guests were already seated at the table. Without any place settings, Janis proceeded to toss hot greasy fish to each of us; she dumped the box of french fries in the middle of the table, and then pushed little piles in our respective directions, all the while, finding everything VERY funny.* [11]

The Revival is Contagious

Since Howard–Browne brought the "blessing" from South Africa to North America, he has been given the ability to "anoint" others so that they can do what he is able to do. The "blessing" is not limited to any one denomination or group of believers. It includes Pentecostals, Nazarenes, Mennonites, Baptists, Methodists, Anglicans, Catholics and many others. The movement has spread internation-

---

[11] Ibid., 14.

ally and churches are being affected all over the world.

Great Britain is "On Fire"

Great Britain was the first to see a whole nation "catch the fire." As with the North American phenomenon, the man who lit the original match was Rodney–Howard Browne. It should be pointed out that the fire was actually transferred to England from the Toronto Airport Vineyard where Elli Mumford, a member of the pastoral team at the South West London Vineyard had spent several hours of "carpet time" in the spring of 1994.[12]

According to Dave Roberts, editor of the British magazine, *Alpha,* and author of the book *The Toronto Blessing,* Mumford's visit to Toronto was transforming: "She had gone there feeling spiritually 'burnt out' and longing for a fresh understanding and vitality in her relationship with Jesus. As she received prayer and encouragement she discovered God anew, much of the time while 'on the carpet' prostrate before God."[13]

On May 24, 1994, Mumford met with several leaders of Holy Trinity Brompton, a charismatic evangelical church in South Kensington. As Mumford prayed at this meeting, "the glory fell." One of the leaders reported to Sandy Millar, the highly–regarded vicar of Holy Trinity Brompton, and it was decided that Mumford would preach the

---

[12] Dave Roberts, *The Toronto Blessing* (Kingsway Publications), 10.

[13] Ibid., 11.

following Sunday morning message at Holy Trinity Brompton.[14]

Sunday, May 29, 1994, was the day the church "caught on fire." After giving her testimony about her "Toronto Experience," Mumford asked the congregation to stand while she prayed that the Lord would bless and give them all that He had. Immediately, people began to laugh hysterically, weep, shake, jerk, bark and roar.[15]

"*The Holy Spirit Hits South Kensington,*" was the front-page headline in the London section of *The Independent,* June 21, 1994. Could such strange behavior be from God? People from the "word-of-faith" health and wealth wing of the charismatic movement had been prophesying a great revival for some time. Was this the real thing?

On June 24, 1994, Holy Trinity Brompton staff member Mark Elsdon-Dew reassured the *Church Times* by saying:

Please emphasize that this is not so bizarre or outrageous that sensible people won't want anything to do with it. We try to show common sense and order, but if it is God it would be awful not to have all that He offers.[16]

At the time of the writing of this book, it is estimated that over 4000 churches throughout Great Britain are holding meetings similar to

---

14 Ibid., 25.
15 Ibid., 13.
16 Ibid., 30.

those of the Toronto Airport Vineyard.[17] Some of the responses of people who have come under "the anointing" in Great Britain are equally as bizarre as the ones in Toronto, as described by Guy Chevreau. In Sidcup Community Church, Dave Roberts reports that

> *someone took ill during the ministry time and the paramedics were called to come to the church. The ambulance men entered the hall and witnessed a scene where dozens were on the floor in various stages of spiritual encounter. "Which one's ours?" they asked, somewhat bemused.*[18]

More amazing are the endorsements that have been made by respected church leaders who originally were skeptical and even critical about the "Toronto Blessing." For example, R.T. Kendall, Minister of Westminster Chapel and highly–respected British Bible teacher, has made the testimony of his conversion to the "Toronto Blessing" public. According to an interview he gave to Wallace Boulton of the British magazine *Renewal,* he stated:

> *I have had to make a public climb down. If you had put me on a lie detector when I first heard about it, and asked me if I thought this was God, I would have said no. Two weeks later I changed my mind. On the evening that Sandy Millar, (vicar of Holy Trinity Brompton) and his staff came to our church, we were about to go home when one of them asked if he could pray for me. I said "Sure, but I must tell you I've been prayed for*

---

17 *Charisma*, "What Is God Doing in Toronto" (February 1995), 20.

18 Dave Roberts, *The Toronto Blessing,* 33.

*many times." I didn't want him to get his
hopes up. Within a minute or so my mind
became so relaxed. The best way I can
describe it was like when I had sodium
penthanol years ago when I had major
surgery.* [19]

The list of prominent church leaders in
England and Scotland who have embraced the
"Toronto Blessing" goes on and on. Colin Dye,
pastor of Kensington Temple, the largest church
in Britain, took the blessing after he was
prayed for by Frances Hunter of the United
States, and fell down laughing on the platform
of his church, unable to stand up after
attempting five times to get up off the floor.[20]

In early July, 1995, I had the opportunity to
attend a Sunday night meeting at Queen's Road
Church in Wimbledon, England which has
become another outpost of the "Toronto
Blessing." The same kinds of phenomena I
observed in Toronto happened there.

What is this power that can cause people to
be persuaded to give over their minds and their
bodies to a person with "the power" to cause
them to lose control? Further analysis of the
roots that provide nutrients for the tree that
bears fruit for the "new wine" will answer the
question.

A Transferable Blessing

John Arnott, senior pastor of the Toronto
Vineyard, received his "blessing" indirectly
from Howard–Browne, through Randy Clark,
Pastor of the Vineyard Church in St. Louis,

---

19 Ibid., 40-41.
20 Ibid., 49.

Missouri. In 1993, Pastor Clark, discouraged
and approaching a nervous breakdown, was
encouraged to attend a Howard–Browne
meeting that was going to be held at Kenneth
Hagin's Rhema Bible College in Tulsa,
Oklahoma.

Emotionally re–charged, after being prayed
for by Howard–Browne, and witnessing the
"power of God" that was being manifested at
this meeting, Clark then took the "anointing"
back to his church. When John Arnott learned
of Clark's experience, he invited him to come to
Toronto and hold a series of meetings
beginning January 20, 1995. The
manifestations which occurred during those
meetings have continued to the time of the
writing of this book.[21]

The secular and Christian media have
expanded the horizons of the movement through
numerous programs and articles. As time
passes, more and more people are being affected
in one way or another. Attitudes toward the
"Toronto Blessing" fall into three categories:
supportive, antagonistic and indifferent. The
latter group suggests there is not enough
evidence to reach an absolute conclusion and
more time is required to determine whether or
not it is from God.

While some claim that their lives have been
refreshed or reformed, others suggest strong
theological concerns. As time goes by, it may be
possible that every church in the world will

---

[21] Paul Carden, "Toronto Blessing Stirs Worldwide
Controversy," *Christian Research Journal* (Winter
1995), 5.

have to make a decision as to what they are going to do with the "Toronto Blessing."

Being a Fool for Christ?

Arnott and other leaders of the Vineyard movement claim that the "Toronto Experience" is part of a "heaven–sent renewal meant for the local church, in order to build up the body of Christ." Arnott also believes that eventually it will overflow into the community and usher in a revival. Arnott stated in an interview:

> *God has told us to give the anointing away to whoever would like it, especially to pastors and elders who can bring it back to their churches. We want them to be the heroes – not us. This is not a Vineyard thing – this is God.*[22]

John Wimber, founder and leader of the Vineyard movement, has also endorsed this "new wave of the Holy Spirit." He believes that what is happening may "readily become a part of the revival we've all longed and prayed for."[23]

Although there are those who are critical of the unusual behavior of people who come under the influence of the "anointing," Wimber believes that these peculiar behavioral responses are to be expected. He stated that "God uses the foolish things of the world to confound the wise."[24]

---

[22] "After the Laughter," *Faith Today* (March-April 1995), 19.

[23] *Ministries Today* (September-October, 1994), 8.

[24] Ibid.

When Randy Clark asked God why He was bringing this unusual behavior to the Toronto Vineyard, God apparently replied to Clark that "He was looking for people who were willing to look publicly foolish for the honor of His name."[25] As Bill Jackson of the Urbana, Illinois Vineyard has emphasized: "The bottom line is one of control. God wants to know who among his people will be willing to play the fool for his glory."[26]

Paul Cain, another strong promoter of "experience–based" Christianity and a close associate of the Vineyard movement, has also made statements justifying why people act so unusual under the "anointing." Speaking at the Toronto Airport Vineyard, he stated:

> *Well you say they do so many foolish things. Well, let me tell you God has chosen the foolish things of this world to confound the wise and the prudent, and God is going to do that in these last days. He is going to put on display the proud arrogant minds of sophistication in a theological world, and God loves offending the sophisticated, even the theologically sophisticated. He is doing it right here. He's doing it everywhere, and I say come on Lord Jesus, come on Holy Spirit, and make a fool of me. I'm tired of being a fool for the devil and a fool in the world. I want to be a fool for the Lord Jesus Christ.*

---

[25] Bill Jackson, *What in the World Is Happening to Us: A Biblical Perspective of Renewal,* Vineyard (Urbana, Illinois: July 1994), 10.

[26] Ibid., 10.

Let Him do anything He wants to do. Let Him completely undo you.[27]

This is not what God intended to say through the apostle Paul when he wrote that "God uses the foolish things of the world to confound the wise."[28] Although God does use ordinary and unlikely people in unusual circumstances to work out His plan and purpose, God does not expect Christians to act "foolish" in order to be used by God.

The Bible teaches that Christians are to exercise self–control and discipline in their lives. Although there is a scriptural basis to prove that people can come under the anointing of the Holy Spirit and operate various gifts that God gives, the "gifts" that are sought after or manifested today are not only unusual, they are highly–questionable if not extra–biblical. The gifts of the Spirit were given by God to achieve spiritual change, not to entertain Christians.

Unusual Signs

For many, this "new anointing" takes the form of bizarre manifestations. While some appear to be seized with violent shaking or trembling, others fall over backwards, passed–out on the floor. Some appear glued or pinned to the floor as if paralyzed.

Others say that they experience feelings of affection and joy that overpowers them. Some are "struck dumb" so that when they attempt to deliver a verbal testimony, they are unable to

---

[27] Paul Cain, transcript of message "God's Latter Rain," Toronto Airport Vineyard, May 28, 1995.

[28] 1 Corinthians 1:27.

speak a word. Then there are those who laugh uncontrollably, make animal sounds like crowing, roaring and barking. And there are some who even hiss like snakes.

Recently, those who have been "anointed" not only make animal sounds but, they actually behave like animals. In spite of these manifestations, people who have experienced the "blessing" say that what has happened to them has truly "been a touch from God." If the so-called gifts of laughter, shaking, twitching, trembling, barking, and "getting drunk in the Spirit," are truly gifts from God, why do human conduits have to be used as the "bartenders"?

There Are Spiritual Gifts

One of the major things that has divided Christians for centuries, is the subject of whether or not the spiritual gifts, which were clearly part of the New Testament Church, were meant for us today. As with every other controversy, there are always two sides. In the case of the spiritual gifts, there are those who are confident that they are not for us today. On the other hand, there are those who believe that God empowered people of the past with supernatural gifts and these same gifts are available for the church today.

However, the controversy that is raging in Christian circles at the present time, is much more complicated. There are people and denominations embracing the various aspects of the "new wave of spirituality" who had never considered the "gifts" mentioned in the Bible.

The greatest opposition to this movement actually comes from Christians who believe that the gifts of the Holy Spirit are for the

church today. This group believes that the gifts
operate according to God's sovereign plan and
are not dependent on human manipulation or
fleshly orchestration. They argue that
measuring spirituality based upon experience
can be dangerous if extra–biblical teachings
are embraced. The author belongs to this
particular segment of Christianity.

No Room for Criticism

Not everyone who has observed the "Toronto
Experience" believes that it is from God. Some
suggest that people who embrace it risk self-
delusion or deception, which is Satanically-
inspired. To these concerns, John Arnott has
replied: "It's about time the church had more
faith in God's ability to bless us than Satan's
ability to deceive us."[29]

Such a statement cannot be supported
scripturally. If we depart from the authority of
God's Word and measure spirituality based on
our feelings and our confidence that we cannot
be deceived, then Satan may deceive us.

The working of God's Spirit should never be
assessed on the basis of whether or not a person
can fall over backwards, speak in tongues, be
"struck dumb" or heal the sick. Satanic
deception is always a possibility. As Peter
stated of the false teachers and the last days
deception that the church would face: "And
many will follow their sensuality, and because
of them the way of the truth will be maligned"
(2 Peter 2:1-2).

---

[29] "After the Laughter," *Faith Today* (March 1995),
19.

Chapter IV
Experience Driven Christianity

Every genuine believer in Christ wants to see a revival. However, the word *revival* more often refers to believers, not unbelievers. There are some who claim the church is being revived as God pours out His Spirit and Christians are being "filled with new wine." Although Christians can and should be revived by God's Holy Spirit on a daily basis, should Christians spend their time seeking after "signs and wonders" and emotional highs, rather than concentrating on serving their Lord and reaching the lost?

A Formula In Order To Receive?

The "laughing gospel" brings forth great praise and great criticism. Proponents say that it is a gift from God. In order to receive "the gift," people are told that they must "give up control, blank out their minds, and just receive." It is said that "the more one seeks after the experience, the stronger their anointing becomes." Some suggest that

churches that have been flowing in this "move
of the Holy Spirit," tend to receive a greater
measure of the anointing.

On the other hand, those who express
caution about the movement are often severely
criticized. Some have said that if you are not in
agreement with what is happening, you are
"blaspheming the Holy Spirit."

But is this so? What if the message that is
being proclaimed is not from God? What if
humans are manipulating humans? Or worse
yet, what if Satan is manipulating humans in
order to deceive humans? Is it possible?

The idea that it is possible to coach people to
receive or distribute the Holy Spirit is also a
wide–spread belief promoted by those who
endorse the "new wine" theology. Leaders who
have received the "anointing," hold seminar
sessions in order to train the "power people"[30]
(ministry team members) who must have
previously received "the blessing" before they
are permitted to pray for others to receive "the
blessing." Manuals have been written laying
out certain rules and regulations on how to
administer the Spirit with certain hand
gestures, and how to "catch" those who fall over
under the influence of "the blessing," as well as
specific instructions on how to pray.

During a question and answer period at a
conference attended by pastors and church
leaders from Canada, Jeremy Sinott, associate
pastor of the Toronto Airport Vineyard, outlined

---

[30] Paul Cain, transcript of message called "The Latter
      Rain," Airport Toronto Vineyard,
      May 28, 1995.

his views on how the ministry team should
pray:

> *Now our model is that we pray very gently.*
> *We have a very high value on gentle prayer.*
> *We may put a hand on a shoulder or the*
> *head, (but) our ministry team knows never,*
> *never, never, to push. Now as we're praying*
> *we'll pray, "Father, give them more of what*
> *you want and desire. You know their hearts,*
> *just fill them with everything you want, bring*
> *any healing you want in their lives. Do what*
> *you want to do Lord, I bless you to do it."*
> *And often there is a response back.*
> *Sometimes tears will begin to flow,*
> *sometimes they will shake...by the way, pray*
> *with your eyes open. Now if you have never*
> *done this before it is weird. But you know, as*
> *you're praying for someone, and you go*
> *through a general kind of prayer, you'll see a*
> *reaction sometimes, tears or a facial*
> *response, or sometimes their bodies will*
> *move a little. Well then, you pray to that*
> *particular area.*[31]

During the Sunday night meeting I attended
at Queen's Road Church in Wimbledon,
England, I observed that the "power people"
never touched the bodies of those they were
praying for. Instead, working in pairs, praying
with their eyes open, they held their hands
slightly above the forehead and behind the
backs of those being prayed for. When I asked a
person who had frequently attended these
meetings what was going on, I was told that
they were focusing the "spirit."

---

[31] Jeremy Sinott, transcript of message at A.C.O.P.
Conference, Yorkdale Holiday Inn,
June 12, 1995.

Pastors who have been to Toronto and returned to their own churches with these new formulas on how to distribute the Holy Spirit, have caused many faithful Christians to wonder what is happening. One man told me that he had recently received a letter from the altar committee chairman at his church informing him that in order for him to continue praying for people at the altar he would have to attend some training sessions. Although he had been praying for people at the altar of this same church for many years, apparently he had to upgrade his qualifications before he could continue.

Those who refuse this "new spirituality" or suggest that the manifestations associated with it are questionable or biblically–unsound, are often referred to as carnal or "spiritually immature." Although it can be pointed out that the teachings associated with this "new revival" place a great deal of emphasis on experience as a means of sensing or feeling the presence of God, criticisms based upon the Word of God are almost always skirted, or various arguments are given explaining why it has to be from God.

Can Good Fruit Be Bad?

Many proponents of this movement suggest that the proof that the "blessing" is from God is because of the "good fruit" that so many have experienced. Some people claim that they have fresh feelings of love. Others say that fear, depression and anxiety are gone. Some marriages have been healed, and others are "on fire for God." However, it can be pointed out that both Mormons and New Agers experience similar feelings and experiences. Does it necessarily follow that what appears to be good fruit, at least for the time being, proves that the source of the fruit is from God. The way to inspect the fruit is to see if it is still good after a much longer period of time.

On one occasion, Jesus talked about checking the fruit and determining its goodness by the principle of first checking the vine to see whether or not it was from the right tree. In Jesus' own words:

> _Abide in Me, and I in you. As the branch cannot bear fruit of itself, unless it abides in the vine, so neither can you, unless you abide in Me. I am the vine, you are the branches. He who abides in Me, and I in him, he bears much fruit; for apart from Me you can do nothing. If anyone does not abide in Me, he is thrown away as a branch and dries up; and they gather them, and cast them into the fire, and they are burned. If you abide in Me, and My words abide in you, ask whatever you wish and it shall be done for you. By this is My Father glorified that you bear much fruit and so prove to be My disciples._[32]

Although the promoters of the "Toronto Blessing" are always willing and ready to give testimony about all of the good things that they have seen take place in peoples lives, there are equally as many horror stories that can also be related. Although the claim is made that the blessing is impacting all of Christianity and that many are coming to the Lord, there are also numerous reports about families, churches and fellowships being divided, because of the unwillingness of doubters of "the blessing" to

---

[32] John 15:4-8.

"catch the fire." One pastor reported to me that a long–standing member of his congregation who was one of the greatest servants he had, claimed that he was leaving the church, because "God was elsewhere."

While visiting Great Britain, where the movement has impacted an entire nation, the reports of "good fruit" going bad are plentiful. One young woman who had experienced "the blessing" in its early stages, was now terrified to return to the same church. At her last encounter on the floor (carpet time), she had experienced an overpowering fear. When she came to her senses, she recognized the ministry person praying over her was a woman in the church who had been recently released from a psychiatric ward.

Others told me of entire churches that had split and only a few of the elders had remained. Formerly, the church was involved in reaching out to the poor and needy in a "soup–kitchen" style of ministry. When the "new wine" started to intoxicate their members, their ministry priorities changed and everyone wanted to be empowered.

Another woman told me that her church no longer cared for the hurting. Her sister had just died of cancer, and her mother had recently been diagnosed with the same cancer. One night after the Sunday evening service, as she was feeling down and depressed, she asked the woman sitting next to her if she would pray for her. The woman responded that she "couldn't do so right then." She had to go forward herself and be prayed for to "get the blessing."

When skeptics suggest that the phenomena associated with the "laughing revival" are not scripturally–based, the supporters argue that not everything associated with the Spirit can be biblically understood. They say that there is nothing in Scripture which specifically forbids these activities, so we should not forbid them. After all, they continue to debate, "we should never put God in a box."

There are others who attempt to justify what is happening by saying that they have placed their complete trust in the leaders of this movement and that it is virtually impossible for these trustworthy Christians to be deceived. One person I met said that he did not believe Christians could be deceived because Jesus said in Matthew 24:24: "if possible, the elect could be deceived." This, he said, proves that Jesus Himself said it was impossible for a Christian to be deceived.

An elementary lesson in Greek reveals this is exactly the opposite of what Jesus was teaching. The Greek meaning of the word "if" in this context is used to speak of things not merely probable but, rather certain and dependent on no condition.[33]

There is no question that God can do whatever He wants to do, and do it whenever and however He wants to do it. The question is, can Satan masquerade himself to do things we think "are of God" when actually they are not? For example, can Satan create a problem, and

---

[33] Spiros Zodhiates, *The Complete Word Study Dictionary* (Chattanooga, TN: AMG Publishers), 504.

then provide a solution for the same problem, which seems to be from God, when actually it is not? There are numerous, documented emotional and physical healings that have occurred in this way. Are healings and miracles a safe way to measure or sense the presence of God? Should we be more cautious of what we believe is from God, when it is based upon experience alone?

Beware of False Teachers

While there is some truth in the arguments used to support the new movement, truth tainted with error is still error. A false teacher or a false prophet is dangerous when they are able to convince their followers that they have "all the truth." Testimonies, "signs and wonders" and personal experiences should never be held as superior revelation to the written Word of God.

It is clear from the Scriptures that the Holy Spirit is given to believers for the purpose of giving them boldness and wisdom for witnessing. However, to say that there are certain methods or techniques not found in the Bible that release the power of God when administered by human beings, is blas—phemous.

Where in Scripture does uncontrolled, hysterical laughing during the preaching of the Word of God ever occur? Can a man become a "Holy Spirit bartender" and disperse the Spirit of God whenever and wherever he says "be filled"?

The time has come for believers to boldly proclaim the importance of getting back to a balance between the Spirit and the Word. Jesus said:

But when He, the Spirit of truth, comes, He will guide you into all the truth.... He shall glorify Me: for He shall take of Mine, and shall disclose it to you.[34]

We must recognize that anyone can be deceived. God has given us His Word. He also promises to give us the wisdom and the grace to be able to discern what is truth and what is not. The choice to be obedient to His Word is up to us.

---

[34] John 16:13-14.

Chapter V
Beyond the Limits

Christians often talk about a balance when it comes to the subject of the Spirit and the Word. Some Christians are criticized because their understanding of God is too intellectually–based or entirely centered around their view of the Bible. At the other end of the spectrum, some Christians rely on what they believe is the moving of the Spirit and ignore the Bible as their guideline to test experience. Which view is correct, or is there a balanced position?

Orderly Deadness or Deadly Disorder

Everyone knows that throughout the body of Christ, there is a wide spectrum of how people emotionally respond to God. There are those who worship Him quietly and reverently. There are those who worship with exuberance and much joy. To label one version of Christianity as spiritually superior to the other, is not justifiable. The Bible teaches that there is room for both, and both are biblical.

However, today, one of the earmarks of the "new spirituality" is the claim that there are far too many churches missing out on the "new wave" because they are too dead or not open to the "new things" that God is doing. In order to be a part of this "new revival," a sense of disorderliness must be entertained.

Consider the following comparison of two very different church styles as presented by Jeremy Sinott, associate pastor with the Toronto Airport Vineyard:

In the church or churches that I had been involved in, there was what I call the order of the graveyard. Now you may have noticed, those of you who hang around graveyards, they are very neat places you know, the grass is always clipped, straight rows, flowers all over the place. But you quickly understand that there's deadness – but it's orderly. Orderly deadness. We also have this thing called order in the nursery – you walk in and you see there are a bunch of toys on the floor here, and there's a diaper pail with smelly diapers in this corner, and this kid is crying, and this kid has his hands around this kid's neck, and... this is order? But you go to the mom and say: "Do you have order in your nursery?" She'll always say, "Yes, there's a routine here, there are parameters, nobody dies in my nursery, nobody dies." Now I kind of shake my head and say, "That's not the kind of order I like. I like things more orderly." But the key thing we look at – there is life. O.K.? I've been involved in far too many churches where there has been the order of the graveyard. It's been real safe but I want to see the order of the nursery.[35]

The analogy that Sinott has used seems to imply that there is some benefit in a disorderly style of Christianity. It also seems to suggest that orderliness is safe, while being disorderly opens the door for new and wondrous things that God can do, although on the surface we might think that it is unusual behavior.

However, by going this route, there is a great danger of opening the door to anything and everything in the name of God. Consider the following reasoning Sinott uses to justify an "experience–based Christianity" that is not based on the whole council of God's Word:

We read in the book of Samuel– here's Saul chasing David to kill him. On the way God's Spirit lands on Saul. Now there's no way anyone can convince me that Saul was praying and said, "Lord, you know I'm on my way to kill David, the one you love. I'm going to kill that kid. Fill me with your Holy Spirit." I can't be convinced. So here he is on the way to kill David and God's Spirit lands on him. He begins to prophecy. He lies down on the ground. He takes off his clothes. Now who would be the first to say if someone did that in your church, "that's God." Not me! And yet there is an account of what we think is bizarre behavior going on and it was God. And so we began to expand our horizons and the box that we kind of place God in, and we say, "Oh Father, oh God, oh God, oh

---

[35]   Jeremy Sinott, transcript of message at A.C.O.P. Conference, Yorkdale Holiday Inn, June 12, 1995.

*God, I give you permission in your church to
do whatever you want.*[36]

A theology based on a single experience
from the Bible to justify all experiences as
blessings from God is ludicrous. Such a view
not only takes God out of a box, it opens a
Pandora's box that can be filled with unlimited
deception.

The Word is True

The Bible states that God has given us His
Word as a guideline so that we can determine
what is truth and what is not. As the Psalmist
wrote:

*From Thy precepts I get understanding;
therefore I hate every false way...The
unfolding of Thy words gives light; it gives
understanding to the simple...Let my cry
become before Thee, O Lord; give me
understanding according to Thy Word.*[37]

Jesus placed a high priority on the validity
of the Word of God when He said "Thy word is
truth."[38]

Paul, who had encountered Holy Spirit
experiences on many occasions, was adamant
about using the Bible as our standard to
determine the truth. As he told Timothy, "All
Scripture is inspired by God and is profitable
for teaching, for reproof, for correction, for
training in righteousness."[39]

---

[36] Ibid.
[37] Psalms 119:104, 130, 169.
[38] John 17:17.
[39] 2 Timothy 3:16.

The Spirit is a Guide

The Bible also teaches that God has given us His Spirit to guide us to truth and to anoint our lives and ministries with the power we need to be effective witnesses. Jesus said, "Thy word is truth," but He also said, "The Spirit will guide you into truth."[40]

The Bible also teaches that without God's Spirit our human efforts are futile: "Not by might, nor by power, but by my spirit, saith the LORD."[41] God certainly wants to use us, but without our recognizing that there is a balance between His Word and His Spirit, we will not be obedient by living according to His will.

When we get out of balance, we need to get back on the scale. Sound, biblically–based faith in God and His Word should never be over-powered by a synthetic, hyper–induced faith driven by experience.

Doctrine is Biblically–based

Christianity is a reasonable faith that should be based upon scripturally–supported doctrine. Although there are no formulas or equations, we should be able to present Christianity to believers and non–believers intelligently and understandably.

Christian doctrine should never be based on emotion or determined upon feelings alone. Feelings and emotions can be wrong. The Bible must be our basis for truth, not someone's testimony.

---

[40] John 16:13.

[41] Zechariah 4:6.

By our own intellect, we are not able to comprehend all that is in the Bible. Should we accept everything that is claimed to be of God, just because someone said that they believe it to be so? As Paul told Timothy,

> *Be a good servant of Jesus Christ, constantly nourished by the words of the faith and of the sound doctrine which you have been following. But have nothing to do with worldly fables fit only for old women. On the other hand, discipline yourself for the purpose of godliness.*[42]

Paul's words for Timothy are appropriate for every believer today. We must make every effort to pay heed to the full council of God.

---

[42] 1 Timothy 4:6-7.

Chapter VI
Extra Biblical Revelation

There are many Christians in the world today who say that they hear directly from God. They know it is God because of the emotional experiences they are feeling. In some cases, these same people say that the Spirit has told them to do or say something but, their actions do not line up with the Bible. Should we just sit back and ignore what is happening or should we stand up and proclaim what the Bible has to say about these things?

Strange Testimonies

There are many personal testimonies today claiming what God is saying and doing. Some of the outward manifestations are so bizarre it seems impossible that these things could be happening. Many who have experienced them are convinced that they have had an encounter with God.

A Christian man I met recently, testified that he went into a trance when he was touched on his forehead and then he went "completely out of it for hours." A women I met said that she had "laughed uncontrollably all through the Sunday morning message" after the pastor had told the congregation to "get drunk in the spirit." When she finally stopped, she was embarrassed and confused; however, she was quite certain it must have been God that made her interrupt the service.

It is reported that people behave like animals when they are overcome by the spirit. Opinions vary widely on the origin of these animal sounds. Many reject them as demonic. Others contend that they are simply a fleshly response.

In the British magazine *Alpha,* Pastor Marc Dupont, from the Toronto Vineyard, mentioned that he has had some difficulty in determining whether or not these animal noises are from God. He described the situation when he prayed for one particular individual. At first, he thought the man might be demon–possessed when he began to roar like a lion. He eventually decided that the man was actually uttering a "prophetic symbolic act," that signified that the Lion of Judah would be triumphant.[43]

John Arnott also thinks that animal behavior in church services has prophetic significance. He admits that sometimes it brings confusion and there are serious questions as to what should be done when it gets out of control. At a pastors meeting, he described some of the problems that occurred, as well as a possible solution. Arnott stated:

---

[43] "What Is God Doing in Toronto?" *Charisma* (February 1995), 25-26.

> Now we are starting to see people prophetically acting like lions and oxen and eagles and even warriors. We had a phone call one time and (the caller) said: "One of our congregation has been acting like an eagle flying around the room. We can't get them to stop, what do we do?" And we thought – you know – throw a rabbit out in the middle of the floor and maybe they'll come down.[44]

John Wimber, a strong promoter of "experience–oriented" Christianity, takes a more conservative position than the Toronto Vineyard pastors with regards to Christians acting like animals. He stated:

> There is nothing in Scripture that supports these kinds of phenomena that I can see, and I can't think of anything throughout the church age that would. So I feel no obligation to try and explain it. It's just phenomena. It's just people responding to God.[45]

Although Wimber may think that people who behave this way are simply responding to God, and that it should not be discouraged because the Bible is silent on the matter, such justification is absurd. Is it possible that the "Toronto Blessing" is not a blessing at all?

---

[44] John Arnott, transcript of Pastor meeting, Toronto Airport Vineyard, October 19, 1994 - borrowed from *Defending the Faith,* January-February 1995, Calvary Chapel Tigard, Oregon.

[45] "What Is God Doing in Toronto?" *Charisma* (February 1995), 26.

"Christian" Television?

Nationally–broadcast "Christian" television programs often blaspheme God by crediting the Holy Spirit with weird and foolish actions. In order to defeat the devil one night, a female Bible teacher told all those attending her meeting that they should take off their shoes. She then had them write the word Satan on the bottom of their shoes, put their shoes back on their feet, then hop up and down, thus stomping out Satan.

On another program, a "faith–healer" asked his congregation to remove their wallets from their pockets and hold them high up in the air. He then cast "the evil–devourer" out of their wallets before the offering was taken.

An Unholy Alliance

Recently, on Trinity Broadcasting Network, a woman gave her testimony about her near–death experience. The well–known Christian host who was interviewing her, listened intently as she spoke.

The woman said that she had met Jesus after she had died, and Jesus appeared to her as a "white light." Jesus told her that she would return to Earth where she would have a ministry to tell people about this experience. She described the "white light" as the "force." She said that this "force" was the same "force" that is mentioned in the movie *Star Wars*.

The host agreed by nodding enthusiastically. This woman, a Mormon, has written a book describing her experience.[46] It

---

[46]   T.B.N. Television Network, February 15, 1995.

has been documented that the Mormon Jesus is Quetzalcoatl – the "feathered serpent" – the son of Venus, to whom thousands of humans have sacrificed their lives.

Jesus warned about false teachers and false prophets who would use His name but, would not be genuine followers. It is possible to masquerade as a follower of Jesus but, actually follow a counterfeit Christ.

Experience Without the Word

In Australia recently, I was scheduled to speak at a Sunday morning service. My topic was "The Coming One–World Religion." When we arrived at the church, the pastor's wife informed us that the message portion of the service had been canceled because "God was doing a new thing" in their church on this particular Sunday morning.

As I sat in the back row observing "the new thing," I was approached by a male member of the church who welcomed me and said that he was looking forward to the subject matter that had been advertised in their bulletin. When I told him why I was not speaking, he went up to the platform and talked to the pastor's wife.

Once again she approached me, this time indicating she would allot me twenty minutes for teaching. Following my twenty–minute message explaining the New Age movement from a biblical perspective, I sat down. Two–thirds of the congregation came up to me afterwards and asked if I would teach them further. They all had family members who were in the New Age movement and did not know what to do.

Where is the scriptural basis for this "new wave of the Holy Spirit" that so many claim is beginning to sweep the world? Is Satan's ability to deceive us no longer a factor?

Many of the things that are happening in the name of Christianity today, border on the "Simon says" kind of behavior practiced by the cults or implemented by hypnotists who work with occultic powers. Has the time come to stand up against this kind of foolishness and get back to the authority of the Word of God which we know to be sound and true?

Chapter VII
Measuring the Experience

There are many people today who are willing to accept an "experience-based Christianity" as the foundation of their faith. Those who have had these experiences often look upon those who have not as people who are too analytical or too critical to be open to the moving of the Holy Spirit. But it can be demonstrated that both Christians and non-Christians can have the same spiritual experiences. How do we then measure what is of God and what is not?

It Was God?

Recently, I read a personal testimony by a young man who wrote about a spiritual blessing he claimed that he had received. By the very words of his testimony, it was obvious that he believed that his experience was a genuine encounter with God. From that point on, he said his life was never the same.

These are the words that the young man used to describe his divine rendezvous: "Immediately I was seized upon by some power which entirely overcame me, as to bind my tongue so I could not speak. I saw a pillar of light over my head, above the brightness of the sun, which descended gradually until it fell upon me."

Shortly after the light had fallen on him, he saw two heavenly beings. One of them spoke in an audible voice and called the young man by his name. Finally, the young man said, "he came to himself again after having been laid out flat on my back on the ground." Several days later, the young man decided to share his spiritual experience with others. To his surprise, the Christians he talked to, told him that what he had experienced was not biblically–based and actually "was of the devil." The young man said he soon realized that his experience "had excited a great deal of prejudice against him" by people who claimed they believed the Bible. He continued: "I was even bitterly persecuted by some."[47]

The "True Church"

Perhaps you know of someone who has had a similar experience. The previous testimony sounds quite familiar to some who have recently encountered what has been called the "Toronto Blessing." However, the testimony just described actually occurred in the spring of 1821. The location was the "Sacred Grove" near Palmyra, New York. The young man who gave the testimony was Joseph Smith, the founding father of Mormonism.

---

47 Excerpted from Joseph Smith History 1:3-75, and *History of the Church of Jesus Christ of Latter-day Saints* (Deseret Book Company, 1967), 1:2-79.

Joseph Smith claimed he had other spiritual encounters which provided additional revelation that Mormons consider to be a necessary addition to the Bible. The Latter–day Saints also believe that the angel Moroni was a heavenly messenger sent from God to help restore the "true gospel" before Jesus returns.

Although much of what Mormons talk about sounds biblical, Bible–believing Christians know that the Mormon belief is not Christian. It is a religion professing the name of Christ but, by its own definition is antichrist because it professes that men can become gods.

To my knowledge, no evangelical Christian has publicly claimed a visitation from the angel Moroni. However, current claims by some promoters of the "new spirituality" indicate that this would not be an impossibility. Experienced–based Christianity has the potential to lead evangelical Christians down the same deceptive path. Perhaps time will tell whether or not it will happen.

There is a Price to Pay

Mormons and Christians who claim that they believe in the authority of the Bible, should read the Bible, to see what it states about revelation that comes out of experience–oriented encounters that are not biblically–based. As Paul stated to the Galatians:

> *I am amazed that you are so quickly deserting Him who called you by the grace of Christ, for a different gospel. But even though we, or an angel from heaven, should preach to you a gospel contrary to that*

which we have preached to you, let him be accursed.[48]

The Scriptures seem to be very clear that preaching a different gospel other than "Christ crucified for our sins" is heresy. Is there any doubt that experiential revelation contrary to the Word of God fits into this category?

---

[48] Galatians 1:6-9.

Chapter VIII
Deceiving Spirits

If the Holy Spirit is embracing the bride with a new affection, and there is a "new wave of the Holy Spirit" bringing about a "paradigm shift"[49] that causes an intimacy with God never before experienced, what is next? Will uncontrollable, hysterical laughter, shaking, shouting, trembling and behaving like animals eventually become too boring and mild. Is this present trend a passing fad, a move of God, or are people opening themselves up to extra-biblical ideas that may lead them into deception?

Is This the Holy Spirit?

It can be documented that much of the "holy laughter" phenomenon can be directly or indirectly traced to Rodney Howard-Browne. Howard-Browne's actions and beliefs often exhibit bizarre, unscriptural behavior. On one occasion, I heard him speaking on the Trinity

---

[49] A New Age term meaning an elevation of or new level of consciousness.

Broadcasting Network, and he admonished people who were praying at an altar to "stop praying and begin to laugh like all of the others...pray at home – this is a time to be filled with laughter."

In the August 1994 issue of *Charisma,* Howard–Browne was quoted as saying: "One night I was preaching on hell, and laughter hit the whole place. The more I told people what hell was like, the more they laughed." On another occasion, Howard–Browne said:

> *I'd rather be in church where the devil and the flesh are manifesting than in a church where nothing is happening because people are too afraid to manifest anything... And if a devil manifests, don't worry about that, either. Rejoice, because at least something is happening.*[50]

So the question is, what is happening in these meetings where these strange manifestations are occurring? If it is not found in the Bible, what proof do we have that is from God?

It is true that a person who is convicted of sin may laugh or cry when released from the guilt and condemnation they have been under after praying a prayer of repentance. But there is no biblical evidence that barking or roaring or hysterical laughing will occur after someone like Rodney Howard–Browne proclaims: "be filled...ho, ho, ho, ha, ha, ha, ha, ho, ho."

---

[50] Rodney Howard-Browne, *The Coming Revival,* (Louisville, Kentucky: R.H.B.E.A. Publications, 1991), 6.

These kinds of manifestations have been historically attributed to demonic spirits, not to the Holy Spirit. To such a statement, the supporters of "holy laughter" disagree. They claim that similar manifestations occurred during the Welsh Revival and the Jonathan Edwards "Second Great Awakening" era, and that it proves it is of God. However, the unusual manifestations that occurred in those days had their supporters and critics. Even Jonathan Edwards and the Puritans were not always in favor of some of the manifestations that occured. According to Richard Lovelace of Gordon–Conwell Seminary in Massachusetts:

> *They (Jonathan Edwards and the Puritans) had a saying that when the sun shines on the swamp, the mist rises. Human nature is full of gross impurities, possibly demonic in nature, that comes out when the gospel goes in. In my own reading of the frontier gospels, that's what you had going.*[51]

So what standard do we have to test whether or not this "new wave of the Holy Spirit" is from God? Does the Word of God allow it? Do perceivod results or outward signs support it as a move of God? Apparently Howard–Browne is so convinced that he has confidently stated "The proof that this is a move of God is that when I leave, it doesn't stop."[52]

Satan – The Serpent – The Deceiver

How closely can Satan counterfeit the real thing? Was this why Jesus was concerned when

---

[51] *Charisma* (August 1994), 26.

[52] Ibid., 31.

the multitudes followed Him only for signs and wonders?

New Age authors Christina and Stanislov Grof, in their book *The Stormy Search For Self,* describe how strange behavior can be triggered by an advanced spiritual leader or guru. The Grofs state that:

> *individuals involved in this process might find it difficult to control their behavior; during powerful rushes of Kundalini energy (the serpent force) people often emit various involuntary sounds, and their bodies move in strange and unexpected patterns. Among the most common manifestations are unmotivated and unnatural laughter or crying, talking in tongues and imitating a variety of animal sounds and movements (page 78–79).*

An Anointing

To most Christians, the occultic connections previously described are blatantly obvious. But, what about other metaphysical ideas that bombard us today.

For example, in the April 1995 issue of the *American Journal of Nursing,* an article called *Discover the Healing Power of Therapeutic Touch,* clearly promotes an eastern world view of God. The author, Rochelle Mackey, describes how therapeutic touch is a technique that allows the practitioner to focus the "energy of the universe" (called prana) upon a recipient. In order for an ordinary person to become a conduit of this "energy flow," they must become "centered." "Centering" is a process whereby you essentially blank out your mind by relaxing through breathing and visualization techniques.

According to Mackey, "when you use therapeutic touch, you're not using your energy. You're simply the conduit through which a healing universal energy is directed toward the recipient."[53] She claims that the recipient does not need to believe in therapeutic touch or be conscious to receive it.

As I watched the focusing and waving of the spirit by the hand gestures of the Queen's Road ministry team in England, I wondered if I was observing the exact same thing. Can believers be conduits of the unholy "spirit" if they have opened themselves up to the fallen spiritual realm? According to 1 Samuel 15:23, rebellion against the known will of God is identical to the sin of witchcraft.

In addition, therapeutic touch produces more than just physical healing. According to Mackey, "The recipient may experience emotional and spiritual growth as well as physical improvement. Your view of life and your priorities may change. You may become more appreciative of nature or your role in life may seem more apparent. Many practitioners of therapeutic touch believe that it not only enhances their nursing abilities, but also prevents career burnout."[54]

It is interesting to note that there are many Christian leaders today saying something very similar. At the point of burnout or deep emotional stress, the "Toronto Experience" has healed their lives and ministries.

---

[53] *American Journal of Nursing* (April 1995), 27.
[54] Ibid.

Is the Holy Spirit an "It" or a Person?

Supporters of the "Toronto Blessing" often face their critics by stating that they are simply not open to the Holy Spirit, and because of their caution, they will miss out on "it." However, those who are concerned about the extra–biblical practices of the supporters of the "Toronto Blessing" say that the Holy Spirit should never be called an "it" because the Holy Spirit is a Person. So is this "it" an "it" or is it a Person?

While observing the "ministry time" at a number of churches operating under the so–called anointing of the "Toronto Blessing," I made a number of observations that troubled me. When praying for people to receive the "experience," very seldom did I see the actual "laying on" of hands. Instead, the "prayer people" passed their hands over various parts of the recipients body, often waving and fluttering their hands or scooping the air as if they were able to transfer some sort of invisible force that could be focused or tossed around.

When I asked members of the "ministry teams" administering this "blessing" about these strange movements, I was told that they were conduits of the "spirit," merely "focusing" His power. When I inquired how to become part of the ministry team, I was told that the prerequisite was to have previously received the "anointing," which they often referred to as "it." One person told me that they had to have been on the floor at least twenty times.

The reference of the Holy Spirit as an "it" also troubled me. When talking to a pastor in Toronto, he told me he was going to preach a sermon on the "Toronto Blessing" titled "The

Mysterious It." On another occasion, I heard Richard Roberts, interviewed on a video called *Rumors of Revival*, say that he had received the "gift of laughter," which he also called the "it" experience.

In the Hindu world view, there is a spiritual power called "shakti" which is a force that is transferable from those who have it to those who do not. Gurus and their top disciples can give it away. The "holier" you are, the more you have experienced the force, and the easier it is to give it to others. Many well-known practitioners of the "shaktipat" have sat with large crowds of their devotees, waved their hands and people have collapsed in ecstatic laughter. When Rajneesh, the deceased cult leader of Oregon, touched his followers, they convulsed in laughter, shook uncontrollably and passed out. The recipients said they all felt such intense peace and joy.

But, you say Satan can counterfeit all of the things that God can do. Maybe so, but God never calls Himself an "it." Some who transfer the "Toronto Blessing" do

We know that God performs miracles, signs and wonders, can heal, and that Satan can counterfeit God. This is not the issue. The issue is – how do we know that the experience we have received is from God. God's Word is our only guide when it comes to emotional experiences.

My greatest concern for people living in these important days is that they will not be deceived – and that includes myself. Is not every human being vulnerable? Perhaps the time has come when we measure our experiences based upon the Word rather than modifying the Word to fit our experiences. If we do not, then indeed, we may be deceived.

Chapter IX
The Roots of the Vine

Many promoters of the "new wine" theology suggest that they have observed the fruit and it is good. Others caution about superficially evaluating the fruit because they know something about the vine upon which the fruit is being born. Building our theology on extra–biblical ideas, in spite of what may appear to be initially beneficial, can be catastrophic, some say. Is it reasonable to check out the roots of this present movement to see if that will give us any clues?

Jesus on False Prophets

Jesus' "sermon on the mount" is one of the most well–known and quoted portions of the Bible. In this portion of Scripture, Jesus talked about the importance of being disciples to the world, personal relationships, giving, prayer, fasting, a cure for anxiety, judging others, and how not to be deceived.

The warning Jesus gave regarding how subtle deception can lead genuine believers astray is certainly worthy of quoting at this point. Jesus said:

> *Beware of the false prophets, who come to you in sheep's clothing, but inwardly are ravenous wolves. You will know them by their fruits. Grapes are not gathered from thorn bushes, nor figs from thistles are they? Even so, every good tree bears good fruit; but the rotten tree bears bad fruit. A good tree can not produce bad fruit, nor can a rotten tree produce good fruit. Every tree that does not bear good fruit is cut down, and thrown into the fire. So then you will know them by their fruits.*[55]

It is important to assess what Jesus is saying in these verses. Although in most cases, fruit inspection can be done from afar by recognizing that the fruit we see must match the appropriate tree, there will be cases when the fruit appears to be good, when actually it is not. As every tree has a root system which lies below the surface of the ground and gathers moisture and nutrients from the soil, it might be beneficial to check out the root system, as well.

Latter Rain

Properly documenting and tracing the complete history of the "new wine" theology back to its roots is beyond the scope of this book. There are other books and authors who have spent years in researching and exposing the roots of this tree. My purpose is to show that the roots of this present movement draw nutrients from very questionable soil. You must make your own decision as to whether or not this soil contains any hazardous materials.

---

[55]   Matthew 7:15-20.

In June, 1995, I attended a meeting at the Toronto Airport Vineyard. Before the meeting, while browsing through the book store, I saw a number of videos for sale of a message called *The Latter Rain* by Paul Cain. The message had been videotaped at the Toronto Airport Vineyard on May 28, 1995. This chapter will explain why I was breathless when I saw this video.

It's Beginning to Rain

Speaking before an exuberant gathering of over 3000 people at the Toronto Airport Vineyard, Paul Cain boldly opened his message:

> *My subject is about the last days latter day outpouring. For quite a while I have been embarrassed to say anything about latter rain, because you are associated and identified with something that people don't seem to appreciate in certain evangelical circles. So I have played it cool and haven't said much about it. But I don't care what they think anymore. All the kind of rain that I know is left is latter rain. I believe we are going to have latter rain and I am looking forward to it* [56]

Perhaps for the vast majority of people who were in attendance at this meeting and for those who watched the videotape at home, the Paul Cain statement meant very little to them. However, for those Christians who had lived through the late 1940's and 1950's, who had observed families, friends, churches and fellowships devastated and divided by the

---

[56] Paul Cain, transcript of message, "The Latter Rain," at Toronto Airport Vineyard (May 28, 1995).

"latter rain" theology propagated at that time, a warning alarm would have been triggered in their heads.

An Earlier "Latter Rain"

The most thorough and well–researched documentation I have seen on the roots of the "Latter Rain" Movement has been done by Albert James Dager, in his four–part series called *Kingdom Theology*. Much of this chapter is based upon his research.

According to Dager, the former "Latter Rain" Movement, originating in the late 1940's, can be traced to Franklin Hall, who established a "major fasting and prayer revival center" in San Diego, California, in the fall of 1946.[57] During this time, Franklin Hall wrote his book, *Atomic Power Through Fasting and Prayer*. This book had a significant impact on a number of other ministries at that time and melded occultic ideas together with Christian terminology. For example, Hall suggested that the prayers of Christians would be hindered if they did not fast, and the prayers of pagans would be answered when they fasted:

Many, if not all American Indian tribes sought revelation of the Great Spirit through Prayer and Fasting. When they had famines, food shortages, lack of rain etc., the Great Spirit was sought through prayer and fasting, and their prayers were answered.[58]

---

[57]   Franklin Hall, *Miracle Word* (Phoenix, AZ: Hall Deliverance Foundation, Inc. Summer 1985), 10.

[58]   Franklin Hall, *Atomic Power with God Through Fasting and Prayer,* 5th Ed. (Phoenix, AZ: Hall Deliverance Foundation, Inc., 1975), 19.

Throughout Hall's teaching, he presented a number of ideas showing his belief that the Zodiac, a study based on astrology, was a valid way of interpreting God's revelation to man. In his book, he stated:

> *In the Zodiacal sign, "Scorpio," which is the eighth sign of the Zodiac, we have a picture of the scorpion with its stinger lifted ready to strike. This is the sign of death, and is supposed to govern the sex area. Just before the sign of the heavens there is a sign of the Judge. Jesus, who is the giver of LIFE, proceeds toward death and pulls the STING OUT OF DEATH. "O death where is thy sting? O, grave, where is thy victory?"* [59]

Another main point of Hall's teaching was in his immortalization theory that stated:

> *"the sleeping, unfoundationally built church" must be awakened to a "real cause and calling that when God's word is completely acted upon and complied with, will result in bringing about the real gushers and torrents of the long, past due, **rain of righteousness**. A rain of **immortality upon the earth** that so many prophets have written about and portrayed in their prophesies."* [60]

Among many of Hall's heretical teachings, was his claim that there is an "Immortal Substance" that comes upon the believer who feeds upon it "from within Christ's new body." Hall called this so–called substance "the shiny

[59] Ibid., 31.

[60] Franklin Hall, *The Return of Immortality*, (Phoenix, AZ: Hall Deliverance Foundation, Inc. 1976), 2-3.

metal–like, Jesus substance."[61] Hall claimed that this "Immortal Substance" could be seen on those who attended his meetings, as a fine, gold and silver sparkling material, emanating from visible "Immortal Heavenly Objects" (IHO's), "Unusual Heavenly Objects" (UHO's), and "Unidentified Flying Objects" (UFO's).[62] Similar to the teachings of the Toronto Vineyard, Hall encouraged open–eyed prayer in order to release "the blessing."[63]

Hall undoubtedly was sincere about his desire to attain spiritual enlightenment, as many are today who look to experiences to measure spirituality. It is clear that occultism mixed with Christian phrases and Bible references has been a stumbling block for many who have been deceived.

William Branham

Another influential "new wine" proponent of the past, whose teachings are being revived by the "new wine" teachers of today, was William Branham. In 1948, influenced by Franklin Hall, Branham changed from a Baptist to a Pentecostal, and taught what he called "God's Seventh Church Age."[64]

Branham literally believed that he was the "angel" referred to in Revelation 3:14 and 10:7, the prophet to the Laodicean Age, the final era of time. Branham believed that his message would

---

61   Ibid., 20.

62   Ibid., 48.

63   Ibid., 10.

64   Albert James Dager, *Media Spotlight-Kingdom Theology* Part I (April-June 1986), 19.

set the world in order, and then Jesus could return. Branham and his followers believed that the true evidence of possessing the Holy Spirit was whether or not you followed "God's prophet," which was Branham.[65]

As with Hall, Branham's teachings were full of heretical beliefs, including his "serpent's seed doctrine" that claimed that Cain was born of an adulterous affair between Satan and Eve, and his Joel's Army idea that claimed that "latter rain" represented the Pentecostal Movement of his day. Branham taught that the Trinity doctrine, a belief that God was three Persons, Father, Son and Holy Spirit, was based upon a Babylonian myth. He claimed that God was one person manifested as three different "attributes."[66] He also taught that the Word of God was given in three different forms: the Zodiac, the Egyptian pyramids, and the written Scriptures.

But Branham's greatest claim to fame was his so-called gift of healing and words of knowledge that he said were channeled through him from "the voice" he identified as an angel.[67] Branham would fall into a trance during healing services, when his angel would work through him. When asked if his healings

---

[65] S.R. Shearer, "The Kansas City Prophets, John Wimber and the Catholic Church" (Denver, Colorado: Antipas Ministries), 10.

[66] William M. Branham, *Adoption* (Jefferson, Indiana: Spoken Word Publications, 1960), 21, 104.

[67] Kurt Koch, *Occult Bondage and Deliverance,* (Grand Rapids, MI: Kriegel. 1972), 50.

were done by the Holy Spirit, Branham replied: "No, my angel does it."[68]

William Branham's life ended abruptly in 1965, six days after his car was hit head–on by a drunk driver. Many of Branham's followers believed that he had truly come in the spirit of Elijah; some believed him to be God, born of a virgin.[69] They expected him to rise from the dead and come back to life after three days. To this date, Branham's body still lies in the grave. His tombstone, a pyramid, can be seen in a graveyard in Jefferson, Indiana. Inscribed on it is his claim that he was "the prophet" for the last days church. Although Branham is dead, his occultic teachings still live on today in those who carry his message.

Branham and Latter Rain

In the late 1940's, Branham had a strong influence on a group from North Battleford, Saskatchewan, Canada, known as the Sharon Brethren. The teachings propagated by this group, known as the "Latter Rain Movement," were based on the heresies of Franklin Hall and William Branham.

One of the most influential members of the Sharon Brethren was Ernest Hawtin who wrote about the revival at North Battleford:

The truth of fasting, was one of the great contributing factors to the revival. One year before this we had read Franklin Hall's book entitled Atomic Power Through Fasting and

---

68   Ibid.

69   David E. Harrell, Jr. *All Things Are Possible,* (Bloomington, Indiana: University Press 1976), 164.

> *Prayer. We immediately began to practice fasting. Previously we had not understood the possibility of long fasts. The revival would have never been possible without the restoration of this great truth through our good brother Hall.*[70]

This "Latter Rain" teaching a combination of the teachings of Hall and Branham, implied that all of the Scriptures relating to the restoration of Israel in the last days were actually for the Church. The followers of this teaching, called "overcomers" or the "Manifested Sons of God," became the perfected and empowered saints who would take dominion over the earth and establish the Kingdom of God.

Another major part of this distorted Scriptural view was a teaching called the Joel's Army doctrine. The "Latter Rain" advocates supported their bizarre "Manifested Sons of God" theory by interpreting the army of locusts in the book of Joel, chapters one and two, as the mighty army of God —the true church (themselves) taking over the planet to prepare for the coming of Jesus.

The Manifested Sons of God

A good indicator that a false doctrine in the church is underway is when a teaching projects that man can be big and powerful while God can be manipulated and made subject to man's

---

70   Richard Riss, *The Latter Rain Movement of 1948 and the Mid-twentieth Century Evangelical Awakening,* (Vancouver, British Columbia: Thesis), 79.

plans and schemes. Clearly the "Manifested Sons of God" idea fits into this category.

A complete study of this heresy and its connection to a current teaching known as "Kingdom Now" theology would be the subject of an entire book. Although few people today who are involved in the "Kingdom Now" world view would be willing to admit their connections with this dangerous heresy of the past, those who have studied the similarities see a strong connection. For example, Albert James Dager sees that the "Manifested Sons of God," the "Kingdom Now," "dominion," "New Wine," and "Latter Rain" ideas have a similar basis and a similar end. In an article called "Latter-day Prophets: The Kansas City Connection," Dager shows the similarities of the Manifested Sons of God teaching with the "Kingdom Message" by outlining:

1) In the latter days, the offices of prophet and apostle will be restored;

2) The prophets will call the Church to holiness and rejection of the world's influences found in the denominational churches. True sonship with God will come through stages of perfection: servant, friend, son, and, ultimately, godhood itself;

3) The apostles will rule the Church through the establishment of independent churches, unaffiliated with the corrupt denominations. The exception would be the denominational churches that leave their covering and join the movement;

4) Through signs and wonders wrought by the apostles and prophets, a world–wide revival will break out, and a majority of the world will

be won to Christ. The signs and wonders will include blessings upon those whom the apostles and prophets bless, and curses upon whom they curse;

5) The revival will come as the result of the Church defeating demonic spirits through prayer, fasting and spiritual warfare, conducted through intense worship and praise, and by rebuking demonic powers and territorial spirits. The restoration of praise and worship is known as the Tabernacle of David, and includes dancing, singing, and exuberant praise in tongues;

6) Those who achieve a certain degree of holiness under the direction of the apostles and prophets will overcome all enemies, including death, and will become immortal. They will complete the conquest of the nations before Christ returns. The conquering is done as Joel's army –an army of immortal beings– bringing judgment upon the ungodly and all who will not accept the authority of the apostles and prophets;

7) Some believe that the second coming of Jesus is in and through the Church. The Church will become the Christ on earth and rule the nations with a rod of iron. Others believe that after the church has taken dominion over the nations, (or a significant portion of the nations) the Church, glorious and triumphant, will call Jesus back to the earth and hand the nations over to Him.[71]

---

[71]   James Albert Dager, "Latter Rain Prophets," *Media Spotlight*, (1990), Redmond, WA, 2-3.

It is obvious that the majority of "Latter Rain" theology can not be supported by sound biblical exegesis, and instead lines up with occultic ideas and methodology. It is a noble idea to live a sinless life without "spot and wrinkle" but, every Bible believer who has an understanding of the grace of God, knows that our hope lies totally in the finished work of the cross and not in any goodness of ourselves.

This teaching seems to appeal to the human weakness of spiritual pride and the lust for power, which has always opened the door for false teachings connected with the occult. There has always been a tendency for a certain sector of Christianity, to want to be able to manipulate or tap into God's power so that they can use the power to help God along.

"Latter Rain," Paul Cain and "New Wine"

It seems almost ludicrous to go over these false teachings of the past to help people understand what is unknowingly being embraced by people today. Perhaps some who are reading this book believe it is just as ludicrous to tie the teachings of Franklin Hall and William Branham to the "revival" that people are talking about today.

However, such a connection is no secret. As Paul Cain stated in his message at the Toronto Vineyard on May 28, 1995, he is no longer embarrassed to talk about "Latter Rain." But, who is Paul Cain?

Paul Cain was born in 1929, in Garland, Texas. He claims that just before his birth, his mother Anna was terminally ill from four diseases: breast cancer, tuberculosis, heart disease, and three, large malignant tumors that prevented her from having a normal delivery.[72]

While on the verge of death, a being appeared to her that she believed to be an Angel of the Lord and said: "Daughter be of good cheer, be not afraid, and you shall live and not die, the fruit of your womb shall be a male child. Name him Paul. He shall preach My gospel as did apostle Paul of old."[73]

At the age of eight, the entity that Cain calls the "Angel of the Lord" visited him for the first time and said: "I want you to preach my gospel as did Paul of old. Open your mouth and I will fill it. You will preach the gospel by binding the sickness and the infirmities of God's people."[74]

According to Cain, he heard this voice on several occasions. Although he believes the Angel of the Lord is actually Jesus, apparently he is not quite sure. He stated: "I heard an audible voice and, of course, often the Angel of the Lord – it might have been the Lord Jesus Christ – but anyway, when he speaks it's rather awesome."[75]

For many years, Cain was a noted member of the "Kansas City Prophets," a group of self-proclaimed prophets with connections to the former "Latter Rain" movement. John Wimber, founder of the Vineyard Movement, has become

---

[72] Terry Sullivant, "Paul Cain: A Personal Profile," *Grace City Report* (Special Edition), 2.

[73] Ibid.

[74] Ibid.

[75] Paul Cain, tape, *The New Breed,* Kansas City, MO, undated.

closely associated with Paul Cain, whose teachings about signs and wonders, miraculous healings, and prophetic utterances line up with his own theology that proposes that God would raise up a multitude of "apostles and prophets" to shepherd God's people through the end times and usher in the Kingdom and the return of Jesus Christ. The Kansas City Prophets were in agreement that the Vineyard Movement would be the group that God would use to accomplish this purpose.[76]

For another perspective of Paul Cain's ministry, we can quote from an article entitled "Prophetic Ministry Arises: Paul Cain Delivers Strong Message to the Church" that states:

> For the 1000 ministers gathered in Kansas City in April, the warning delivered by Paul Cain was strong and clear. The shaking that is to come is greater than anything we have ever seen. Cain explained this was a continuation of the prophecies which began in 1980 when he shared a platform with Kenneth Hagin. At the meeting, Cain operated in a prophetic anointing which included personal messages to ministers with details such as names of associates that he had no way of knowing. Cain preached in healing meetings in the 1950's. Recently he has re-emerged, working closely with Kansas City Fellowships team leader Mike Bickel and John Wimber of Vineyard Ministries International.[77]

---

[76] S.R. Shearer, "The Kansas City Prophets, John Wimber and the Catholic Church" (Denver Colorado: Antipas Ministries), 5.

[77] *Charisma* (July 1989), 27.

The fact that he has "re—emerged" is rather significant in light of the historical pattern I have presented. It can be documented that Cain's mentor was William Branham.[78] In April 1987, Cain met with the leadership of Kansas City Fellowship who received him as a father. Bob Jones, a member of the Kansas City Prophets, referred to Cain's personal ministry as "the terror of the Lord." He also called Cain "the most—anointed prophet that's in the world today."[79]

Although for years Cain was reluctant to publicly talk about his connection with William Branham, now that the "Toronto Blessing" is sweeping the world, he now seems willing to talk about "Latter Rain." In Cain's own words, the time has come for his ministry to shine:

> *So the rain that I have lived for all my life may come in my life time and I am very excited about that. I tell you, I am getting excited these days because the signs are showing and the very air is being charged with praises that are ascending into heaven and forming the clouds that we now we see.*[80]

---

[78] S.R. Shearer, "The Kansas City Prophets, John Wimber and the Catholic Church" (Denver, Colorado: Antipas Ministries), 7.

[79] Bob Jones, tape, *Visions and Revelations*, interview with Mike Bickel (Kansas City, MO: Grace Ministries, Fall, 1988).

[80] Paul Cain, transcript of message "The Latter Rain" at Toronto Airport Vineyard (May 28, 1995).

In case there is still some doubt about the connection with the earlier "Latter Rain" doctrine that taught that Christians would take over the planet in a great and mighty revival before Jesus comes, consider Cain's own words:

> *We are soon to see the day of the Lord's power and people are not going to have to be drafted. They will willingly volunteer for the army of the Lord. You know the time has come when I no longer feel premature in talking about Gideon's army or Joel's army or the last days army – the army of God. There is an army coming, and I am about to tell you that when the power of God is revealed in this army, no one will be drafted, everyone will want to volunteer in the hour of God's power. They are going to come right on in to the day of the Lord's power.*[81]

Is this type of teaching, which is such a prevalent part of the "new wine" theology, biblical? Not every spiritual experience is from God, even though it may be packaged in the name of Christianity. Should we be more cautious and concerned when our experiences do not line up with the Scriptures?

---

[81] Ibid.

Chapter X
A New Man for the New Era

What do people mean when they say that there is a "new wave" of the Holy Spirit taking place in the world today? Does this mean that God is "doing a new thing" as some say? Is a paradigm shift transforming Christians to prepare the way for the return of the Lord? Is a new brand of Christian emerging? Will Christianity take over the world in the greatest revival ever known to man? Or, should we be paying heed to Paul's warnings that the last days will be a time of great deception?

The Spiritually-Elite

As has occurred at other periods of church history, a sector of Christianity is claiming that they have found the way to spiritual enlightenment. As certain manifestations provide the evidence of whether or not one has entered through the door and been awakened, those who refuse to participate or who are skeptical, are considered spiritually immature.

Some go so far as to say that those who do not blindly accept the extra–biblical teachings are holding back revival. For example, Mona Johnian predicted impending doom on those who will not drink deeply of the "new wine." She stated:

> *The question we as believers must ask is this: Will we flow with the plans and purposes of God for this hour or will we hinder revival? I'm concerned that many are in danger of creating a false comfort zone for themselves. By the position they are taking, they are saying, "I'm not sure about this present move. I'm just going to wait and see what happens." But Jesus said, "He who is not with Me is against Me." Pentecost was not, and is not an option. God considers us to be either for or against what He is doing at any given time.*[82]

It is interesting to note that this twisted theological view agrees with a position some evangelical Christians are professing in which they believe God creates "progressively." According to this belief, the sixth day of creation has never been completed and God is still creating.

A new "spiritual man" is now in the process of emerging, some say. They suggest that certain laws, principles and techniques can be tapped into which will help individuals onward and upward on their spiritual journey. Christians will become powerful conduits, able to administer the "anointing" to others. The whole world will turn to Christianity in a mighty revival that will sweep the world. Signs and wonders will be plentiful before Jesus returns to meet His victorious perfect church.

---

[82] *Charisma* (February 1995), 14.

Spiritual Pride

Although many advocates of the "new wine theology" often claim that revivals like the Jonathan Edwards "Great Awakening Era" produced genuine, godly, committed believers, completely dedicated to reaching the lost for the Lord, there are other historical accounts which seem to indicate that not all the enlightened were as saintly as suggested.

For example, Charles Chauncy, who lived during that period, urged caution about personal experience superseding biblical revelation. In his book called *Enthusiasm Described and Caution'd Against (1742),* he defined the "spiritual experience seeker" of his day as:

one who has a conceit of himself as a person favored with the extraordinary presence of the deity. He (the enthusiast) mistakes the workings of his own passions for divine communications, and fancies himself immediately inspired by the Spirit of God, when all the while, he is under no other influence than that of an over-heated imagination.

Chauncy further commented on his observations regarding the spiritual fruit that he and others observed that was the product of a superior spiritual attitude that some were expressing. He stated:

I can't see that men have been made better, if hereby be meant, their being former to a nearer resemblance to the divine being in moral holiness. It is not evident to me, that persons, generally, have a better understanding of religion, a better government of their passions, a more Christian love to their neighbor, or that they are more decent and regular in their devotions to God... What is a grand discriminating mark of this work, is that it makes men spiritually proud and conceited and uncharitable, to neighbors, to relations, even to the nearest and dearest, to ministers in an especial manner; yea to all mankind, who are not as they are, and don't think and act as they do.[83]

Although, we must be careful not to condemn or judge everyone who promotes the "new wine theology" by these same standards or accusations, many of the words and examples that Chauncy chose could certainly apply to some of the statements, actions and behavior of people today.

British author Dave Roberts, in his book *The Toronto Blessing,* presents a detailed overview and a defense of the "new wine" theology in Great Britain. The choice of words that he uses seems to indicate that those who oppose "the blessing" are the division makers. He states:

Division often arises out of impatience and judgementalism, for those who are against a new expression of God's power, and from those who are immature in their expression of enthusiasm for it. Mature believers will respect each other's dignity and will disagree agreeably. Moderation is much more likely to spring from loving, careful but honest dialogue than from a "heresy, deception, doom and gloom" mentality. It was divisive when Paul took a stand against the legalism of the Judeans, but he still had to do it and to act as God commanded.

---

[83] Richard Bushman, *The Great Awakening: Documents on the Revival of Religion*, 1740-45 (Atheneum, New York: 1970), 120.

*Division over principle is unavoidable in our
fallen state.*[84]

Man's fallen human nature, spiritual pride
and insensitivity for others, have always gone
hand in hand. If our professed love for God,
and our own personal agendas separate us from
other believers because of a superior spiritual
attitude that we are the ones who have truly been
"anointed" while those who have not are not, we
may be in for a terrible fall. Those who profess
the "new wine for the new era" may have fallen
into this trap. There is still time to reconsider
and make amends.

Receive or Die?

One of the disturbing teachings that is
beginning to surface in some evangelical
circles is the idea that those who do not embrace
the "Toronto Blessing" are the "unorthodox
ones" who are not willing to "go on with God."
Kenneth Copeland has suggested that those who
refuse to participate in this move may be struck
down and die. He stated:

*One of these days, you may be talking to
someone, asking them how things went at
church last Sunday, and they may say, "Oh it
was great! The glory of God was so strong it
healed ten cripples, opened the ears of
thirty deaf people, cured seven cases of
cancer and killed Brother Bigmouth and
Sister Strife."*[85]

---

[84] Dave Roberts, *The Toronto Blessing* (Kingsway
Publications Ltd), 148.

[85] *Believer's Voice of Victory* magazine (October
1994).

What is this idea that Christians can be struck down and killed if they resist what is called the "move of God?" This sort of teaching that predicts judgment upon opponents of the "new wine theology" has been building for some time. It is a revival of the "Manifested Sons of God" doctrine which also taught that denominational Christianity was Babylon and that only the perfected saints, the "overcomers," would emerge in the end times as the "Chosen of God."

The "New Jerusalem"

As mentioned earlier, the "Latter Rain" teachings of the past replaced all prophecies relating to a "last days Israel" with their own bizarre interpretation of a triumphant endtimes Church. These strange doctrines, rejected as an orthodox view of Christianity, are being revived, and in many cases, without any revision. There are new messengers but, the message is still the same.

A common theme of the "renewal–revival" hype is the idea that "something new is being birthed in the Church" and "God is raising up a mighty army." It is interesting that Toronto, in Eastern Canada, is being equated to Jerusalem, which everyone knows is situated in an entirely different part of the world. Consider the following report given by Dave Roberts in his book, the *Toronto Blessing*:

> Marc Dupont (May 1992), of the pastoral team at the Airport Vineyard in Toronto, has a lengthy vision. In the vision he sees water falling over an extremely large rock. There is a huge volume of water. He believes God is telling him that Toronto shall be a place where much living water will be flowing with

*great power, even though at the present
time both the church and the city are the
big rocks, cold and hard against God's love
and his Spirit. He sees this water flow out
over the plains of Canada and ignite revival.
In July 1993, Dupont, while on a visit to
Vancouver, is touched by a "sense of
urgency." He foresees "power and authority
coming to the church in the Toronto area."
There is going to be a move of the Spirit of
God on the city that is going to include
powerful signs and wonders, such as in the
early days of the church in Jerusalem.*[86]

Consider the following statement from
Master Potter ministries regarding a predicted
world–wide revival for the Church:

*The dry bones of the Church will be revived,
as described in Ezekiel 37 and Acts 2, to
advance the Kingdom of God so we can go
out and restore the bones in the graveyards
of the world.*[87]

The "dry bones" mentioned in Ezekiel 37
refer to Israel and not the Church. A casual
reading of Acts 2 does not mention "dry bones"
at all.

A New Child is Being Born?

Along with the reviving of "dry bones,"
there is mention of the birth of a new
"manchild." In an interview with Pat
Robertson on June 9, 1994, Judson Cornwall
related that Glenn Foster had a vision in

---

[86] Dave Roberts, *The Toronto Blessing* (Kingsway
Publications), 16-17.

[87] Jill Austin, *Master Potter, Prophetic Insights for
the 90's,* "The Great Intruder" (Passion and Fire
Conferences, Summer 1994).

January, concerning himself and Cornwall. Foster claimed that during this vision, the Lord revealed the following:

> *I am now impregnating some of my mature, older ministers with truth... I am choosing my older men because I can trust them to carry that truth to full gestation and have the patience to raise it up once it is delivered... I will bring forth truth that is not being taught and you will be part of it.*[88]

What is this "truth" that is not being taught, that is so necessary for us today? Have previous Bible scholars been slack in their teaching of the Bible? Is there some new revelation that has been overlooked until just recently, that is necessary to empower Christians in the "last days"? Many prominent, "new wine" theologians believe this to be so. John Wimber said:

> *There will be a time where even as Acts 2, suddenly, as they were gathered, in the midst of them, the Lord came and with an anointing beyond anything that has ever been given to man before. Something astounding, so marvelous that God has kept it a mystery as it were, behind His back, and He is about to reveal it. With the judgment of all mankind will come this incredible incarnational endowment of God's Spirit and we will see the Elijah's... this end time army will be made of the Elijah's of the Lord God.*[89]

---

[88] Pat Robertson Interview with Judson Cornwall, 700 Club (June 9, 1994).

[89] John Wimber, speaking at Docklands, England (October 1990), from *Weighed and Found Wanting:*

Well–known TV evangelist and "new wine" enthusiast Morris Cerullo has been foretelling the same kind of "Manifested Sons of God" doctrine for several years. In a video entitled *Manifested Sons of God,* he said:

(Jesus) was the reflection, image and manifestation visibly of all that God has and is. What is God's purpose and plan and objective? Sons and Daughters who will manifest all that God is. Can you imagine the power in your being when you face the devil? You represent all that God is and all that God has.[90]

To assist the people present at this meeting to receive the power that John Wimber says that God has been holding behind His back, Cerullo asked the people to repeat after him:

Everyone repeat after me... God is duplicating Himself in the earth... At last the time has arrived, God is releasing His life through the Body... Today, I am a Son of the all powerful Almighty God... the fullness of the Godhead dwells in me... God has planned for me to be Christ's image on earth.[91]

And consider these words, given as a prophecy by Wallace Hickey:

The Spirit in this very hour says, "don't think you have seen it all as you go in the Holy Ghost way. God is new and He's a growing person as anything that is alive. So you don't

---

Putting the Toronto Blessing in Context, Bill Randles.

[90] Morris Cerullo, video transcript, "Manifested Sons of God" (1991).

[91] Ibid.

*have to work it up or try in our own flesh to
strive. Just let God be God in you as a child,
as a child be. God would will that the whole
of everyone in eternity would be like He is,
never old, ever young, growing, a growing
thing."*[92]

This "new child" and "new thing" that
some call the "paradigm shift" that Christians
are now experiencing, sounds strangely
familiar to me. The Joel's Army, Latter Rain,
Overcomers, and Manifested Sons of God
teachings that were propagated by William
Branham and others some fifty years ago are
alive and well, once again. Only this time, in
the name of Christianity, it is happening in a
wave that is sweeping the whole world.

Man–Made Utopia?

Although there are increasing numbers of
Christians who support the belief that Christ can
not return to Earth until Christians have
"Christianized" the planet, there are others who
suggest that this view is prophetically wrong.
Rather than things getting better and better,
they say that the Bible teaches that the end times
will be a time when things get worse and worse,
and there will be tremendous deception.

The concept of a utopian planet that will be
prepared for the return of Jesus actually has its
roots in a theological position known as
aumillenialism. The Roman Catholic church,
and many of the liberal Protestant
denominations, have espoused this view for

---

[92] Wallace Hickey, speaking at a Rodney Howard-
Browne meeting, aired on Trinity Broadcasting
Newtork (May 1994).

centuries. However, now there are many who call themselves "evangelical" who also believe that Jesus Christ will empower humans to "Christianize" the planet in order that He can return. This concept somehow appeals to man's innate desire to expand his own powers and limit God to our human standards.

Getting With the Flow

To "get with the flow," proponents of the "new wine" theology suggest that it is easy to get involved – just "jump in and let go." Those who are not willing to do so, are "missing out on God's move," or are "closed to the Holy Spirit."

In their book *Holy Laughter,* Charles and Frances Hunter, (known as the Happy Hunters) encourage their readers to let go of their inhibitions and make every effort to be a part of the revival program that they believe will usher in the return of Jesus Christ. Regarding the outpouring of the "new wave of the Holy Spirit," they ask the question:

> Could this be the way God is bringing us into final revival before the return of Jesus? Whether it is or not, we can feel the Holy Spirit moving – and we're going right along with Him! Don't stick your toe in the test water! Don't wait! Jump all the way into the flowing river![93]

To justify their view without having any biblical basis, the Happy Hunters and other enthusiasts of the "new paradigm shift" suggest that one of the prerequisites for the "blessing" is

---

[93] Charles and Frances Hunter, *Holy Laughter* (Hunter Books), 159.

to "open" your mind to what the Spirit might be doing. In this way, there is a much better opportunity to receive. As they wrote in their book:

> *We always need to be completely open to the move of the Holy Spirit and never be so closed that we cannot see that God might be doing something so fresh and new today that there is no way our infinite minds can understand it! Let's just enjoy it and not try to figure out God.*[94]

The Bible does teach that we can not figure out God. In fact, His thoughts, compared to ours, are as high as the heavens are above the Earth. This does not give us the freedom to commit spiritual suicide by opening the door to everything that is claimed to be from God. Once again I repeat, "experience–based" Christianity opens the door to every kind of spiritual deception known to man.

Samuel rebuked Saul by telling him that rebelling against the known will of God was the same as someone who practiced witchcraft. Samuel said:

> *For rebellion is as the sin of divination, and insubordination as is as iniquity and idolatry. Because you have rejected the word of the Lord, He has also rejected you from being king.*[95]

Do these same words provide warning for us today? If Christians willingly reject the authority of Scripture and open themselves up to

---

94   Ibid., 103.
95   1 Samuel 15:23.

deceptive powers, is it possible that they will be deceived?

A Time for Discernment

Although skeptics of the "massive revival theory," believe it is the church's primary responsibility to evangelize the lost, they do not see the whole world accepting Jesus Christ as their Lord and Savior before Jesus returns. In fact, they believe that the Bible teaches that many people claiming to be Christians will actually be deceived at this time. Some say that one of the greatest threats to Christianity in the future, will be Christianity itself –"false Christianity." According to this view, during the last days there will be a departure from the authority of Scripture and a counterfeit revival will occur, merging believers with unbelievers.[96]

Such a union of various religious faiths embraced by people calling themselves Christian, would have never seemed possible a decade or so ago. However, today, such is not the case. "Experience–oriented–faith," coupled with the desire for seeking after "signs–and–wonders," has prepared the ground for an ecumenical delusion that will be the end–times religious system embraced by the antichrist. A global spirituality embracing occultic power is unfolding all over the world today at an incredible rate. Certainly this is a time when we Christians should cling to the Scriptures as never before.

---

[96]   2 Thessalonians 2:3 and 1 Timothy 4:1.

The Cosmic Christ

Paul Cain and others associated with the revived Latter Rain doctrine that is such an integral part of the "Toronto Blessing" spreading around the world, are not the only ones using the book of Joel as to justify the birth of a "new man for a new era." For example, consider the words of former Catholic priest Matthew Fox, now a New Age promoter, in his book *The Coming of the Cosmic Christ: The Healing of Mother Earth and the Birth of a Global Renaissance*. In it, he compares what he sees as about to happen today to the words found in Joel:

> *The mystical awakening that foreshadows a global healing is presented as a cosmic awakening, an awakening to a living cosmology, to a Cosmic Christ alive and vital in all creatures and all humans – young and old, slave and free, male and female. I foresee a renaissance, "a rebirth based on a spiritual initiative," to use M.D. Chenu's definition, as the result of the outpouring of the Spirit. This new birth will cut through all cultures and all religions and indeed will draw forth the wisdom common to all vital mystical traditions in a global religious awakening I call "deep ecumenism." Joel too ends his prophecy with a vision of hope: "When that day comes, the mountains will run with new wine and the hills flow with milk, and all the river beds of Judah will run with water."[97]*

---

97   Matthew Fox, *The Coming of the Cosmic Christ, The Healing of Mother Earth and the Birth of a Global Renaissance* (San Francisco, CA: Harper and Row Publishers), 5.

It is apparent that Fox and those pushing for the new era of spiritual enlightenment suggest that we let go of a traditional view of Christianity and go with the feelings and expressions associated with what Fox calls the "Cosmic Christ." Fox states:

> *I believe the issue today for the third millennium of Christianity – if our earth is to survive into the next century – is the quest for the Cosmic Christ. The movement from the Enlightenment's quest for the historical Jesus to today's quest for the Cosmic Christ names the paradigm shift that religion and theology presently undergo.*[98]

This paradigm shift that Fox and others refer to is part of the great delusion that the Bible foretells will occur before Jesus returns. Fox states:

> *Every theologian must embark on these pathways and awaken them if the theological enterprise is to accomplish its task in our time. This will require a deep letting go of the old paradigms of education and theology. The old wineskins of an anthropocentric, rationalistic, antimystical, antimaterial world view can not contain the new wine of creativity that is exploding wherever minds, and hearts and bodies are being baptized into a cosmology, into the living Cosmic Christ. Perhaps it is time to back huge moving vans up to seminaries, load up the immense theological paraphernalia that has accumulated around the theme of the historical Jesus, and*

---

[98] Ibid., 78.

channel religion's resources in another direction – the quest for the Cosmic Christ.[99]

The Ultimate Delusion

There are many non–Christians in the world today saying we are in the most critical period of history the world has ever known. The next few years are crucial to all of mankind if we are going to survive, they say. Calling this period "a time of transition," man is supposed to emerge from the global pressures that threaten our extinction and become a new and higher being that will lead us onward and upward in the future. Are these utopian promises hopeful and exciting, or could they lead to our demise?

According to many New Age proponents, there is a new baby in the wings. Out of the turmoil, chaos, destruction and disaster that the world is presently experiencing, a new possibility for the Earth and humanity will emerge. As one recent New Age magazine reported:

> *From 1996, right through into the next century, there will be the period of the "pushing" out of the new Child. We really don't know yet what this Child will look like, but the labor has begun as we move towards the New Age.*[100]

Beware of Deception

Although such a grandiose prediction of "a new being" for the future, seems far too ridiculous to ever be embraced by Bible–

---

99 Ibid., 78-79.

100 *Golden Age*, The Magazine for Personal Transformation, (January-February 1995), 33.

believing Christians, spiritual deception does not always come marked with a skull and a cross.

Where does it say in the Bible that to be moved upon by the Holy Spirit, we deserve it or earn it by our actions, by "soaking in His presence," (carpet time) or "glued" to the floor? Is the Holy Spirit an accumulative commodity that "the more often we soak in His presence, the stronger our anointing becomes?" Where does this new doctrine make room for the grace of God? Does God become a cosmic puppet that can be dangled on a string?

Where in the Bible do people worship God with hysterical laughing, shrieking, twitching, howling, hissing or roaring like lions? Although I can not find these things occuring in association with God's Kingdom, the Bible does mention such activity associated with demonic power. As Jeremiah prophesied about how God would deal with the sins of Babylon:

> And Babylon will become a heap of ruins, a haunt of jackuls, an object of horror and hissing, without inhabitants. They will roar together like young lions, they will growl like lions' cubs. When they become heated up I will serve them their banquet and make them drunk, that they may become jubilant and may sleep a perpetual sleep and not wake up declares the LORD. I shall bring them down like lambs to the slaughter, like rams together with male goats. [101]

---

[101] Jeremiah 51:37-40.

It's a Serious Matter

Peter proclaimed that the Scriptures were absolutely true and accurate regarding the subject of the future. He made it clear that we do not have to speculate when it comes to knowing the future when the Bible speaks on the subject. As he said:

And so we have the prophetic word made sure to which you do well to pay attention as to a lamp shining in a dark place, until the day dawns and the morning star arises in your hearts.[102]

Regarding the last days scenario Peter went on to say: "But false prophets also arose among the people, just as there will also be false teachers among you who will secretly introduce destructive heresies, even denying the Master who brought them, bringing swift destruction upon themselves. And many will follow their sensuality, and because of them the way of the truth will be maligned."[103]

Is it reasonable then, that we pay heed to what the Scriptures say about the future? If we do not, then there is a strong chance that we will be deceived.

---

[102]   2 Peter 1:19.

[103]   2 Peter 2:1-2.

Chapter XI
Searching the Scriptures

While an increasing number of Christians around the world today are seeking "the gift of laughter" in an attempt to experience God, hundreds of millions of non–believers are directly headed down the wide pathway to hell. Is this so–called "new wave of the Spirit" really a revival in the church, or is a portion of the church being made ineffective as the rest of the world prepares to burn?

"New Wine" or Old Story

Although some suggest that a "new spiritual man is being prepared," others see this as a sign of the last days when apostasy would abound. Rather than the gospel being proclaimed unto the world before the end comes, many Christians believe that the end can not come until Christians do their part to get the world ready to welcome the return of Jesus by presenting a "glorious church without spot or wrinkle."

This phrase "without spot or wrinkle" is used in Scripture to describe the body of Christ, who have been made righteous and blameless in His sight, as a result of who He is and what He has done.

The "new covenant" or "Kingdom Now" theology being proclaimed throughout many churches today, concerning a great outpouring of power in the last days upon an elite group of believers, is a dangerous eschatological teaching that has no foundation in Scripture. Although the Bible clearly teaches that individuals can have victory over sin and live a victorious life in Jesus Christ, this does not mean that Christianity will take over the world.

Jesus said that the "gospel would be proclaimed as a witness to all the nations and then the end would come."[104] This is beginning to happen now. To say that there will be a massive revival as the majority of the world turns to Jesus Christ as their Lord and Savior, is far from what the Bible teaches.

The "new wine" theology promises its followers a new wave of extraordinary power. It seems that the people who are spiritually desperate, or seek fleshly stimulation in order to "experience" God, or have a shallow understanding of the Word of God, are the ones who most readily embrace the teaching and practices which are contrary to Scripture. Many pastors and teachers today who are part of this movement have failed to feed their sheep and guard the flock against false shepherds and false teachers who have come among the people and found them easy prey.

---

[104]   Matthew 24:14.

Hebrews 5:14 teaches that a sound knowledge of the Word of God brings spiritual maturity that gives believers the ability to distinguish good from evil. The Gospel of Jesus Christ clearly describes who God is and who we are. It is the only way we can come into a relationship with the One who made us. When we come into this relationship, we will have a life–changing experience. The gospel changes lives. As Paul said:

For I am not ashamed of the gospel, for it is the power of God for salvation to everyone who believes.[105]

When miracles and experiences take precedence over the preaching of the cross, then Christianity is no longer a Christ–centered faith. Instead, it becomes a self–centered, flesh–fulfilling, "what's–in–it–for–me" belief, promoting ourselves at the expense of others.

Deception Protection

If there is one factor that would indicate that the end times are unfolding before our eyes, it would be the sign that great deception is taking place all over the world in the name of Christianity. Satan has always been given the subtitle of the "deceiver." Deception is his game. And Christians are not immune.

When it comes to the topic of spiritual deception, the Bible provides a set of rules that all Christians should live by. When one chooses to ignore those rules, there will be consequences. Although Christians have been given God's Spirit so that they can be guided to the truth and be in communion with Him, the

---

[105] Romans 1:16.

devil does everything he can to bombard us with counterfeit signals that our fallen natures are always willing to receive.

We Were Warned

When Jesus was asked what signs would indicate that His return was near, Jesus immediately answered His disciples by saying: "See to it that no one misleads you, for many will come in my name and mislead many."[106] As He continued to list other events that would indicate that His second coming was near, He repeated the warning about deception. He said: "And many false prophets will arise and will mislead many."[107]

Paul continually warned about a last days delusion that would affect believers. He said: "The Spirit clearly says that in later times some will abandon the faith and follow deceiving spirits and things taught by demons."[108] Paul also stated:

For the time will come when men will not put up with sound doctrine. Instead, to suit their own desires, they will gather around them a great number of teachers to say what their itching ears want to hear. They will turn their ears away from the truth and turn aside to myths.[109]

Regarding this same scenario, he continued: "But evil men and impostors will

---

106   Matthew 24:4-5.
107   Matthew 24:11.
108   1 Timothy 4:1.
109   2 Timothy 4:3-4.

proceed from bad to worse, deceiving and being deceived."[110]

Paul also made it clear that the last days scenario would be a time when Satan's power would be manifested in various ways through human vessels. In the second chapter of Timothy, where Paul lays out a list of last days symptoms indicating that the return of Jesus is near, Paul specifically mentions the use of sorcery as a means of manipulating people. He stated:

> *And just as Jannes and Jambres opposed Moses, so these men of depraved mind, rejected as regards the faith, but they will not make further progress; for their folly will be obvious to all, as also that of those two came to be.* [111]

The reference to Jannes and Jambres refers to Exodus 7:11, when these two sorcerers performed signs and wonders by turning a stick into a serpent. Certainly, this would be a miracle to any bystander who observed then, or now. Such events will become quite popular in the future, according to Paul's second letter to the Thessalonians. Regarding the coming man of perdition (the antichrist), Paul wrote:

> *Let no one in any way deceive you, for it will not come unless the apostasy comes first and the man of lawlessness is revealed, the son of destruction, who opposes and exalts himself above every so-called god or object of worship, so that he takes his seat in the*

---

[110] 2 Timothy 3:13.

[111] 2 Timothy 3:8-10.

temple of God, displaying himself as being God.[112]

Paul continues to describe the occultic powers that this man, claiming to be god, will demonstrate:

the one whose coming is in accord with the activity of Satan, with all power and signs and false wonders, and with all the deception of wickedness for those who perish, because they did not receive the love of the truth so as to be saved. And for this reason God will send upon them a deluding influence so that they might believe what is false.[113]

How can any serious Bible–believer miss the warning? If these are the last days, as so many Christians believe, then we should be spending our time and energy reaching out to the lost and warning others what is coming. The Bible states that Satan has blinded the minds of the unbelieving so that they are unable to understand the Gospel. Paul writes:

But even if our gospel is veiled, it is veiled to those who are perishing, whose minds the god of this age has blinded, who do not believe.[114]

Can Satan also blind the minds of believers so that they can actually miss the point of why we are all still here?

---

[112] 2 Thessalonians 2:3-4.

[113] 2 Thessalonians 2:9-11.

[114] 2 Corinthians 4:3-4.

History Repeats Itself

A brief review of history from a biblical perspective reveals mankind has always had the tendency to fall for Satan's lie that man has the potential to have godlike powers. Of course, this was the lie that Satan used to get Eve to make her fatal decision to disobey God. Doubting or rejecting God's Word has been the downfall of every generation.

The history of the children of Israel provides us with another good example of what happens when man goes his way rather than being obedient to God. Although God said that He would bless them abundantly if they were obedient to His Word, we see that they repeatedly rejected the truth, went their own way and followed the pagans by participating in the rebellious worship of pagan gods.

Although Christians are familiar with these examples and are aware of the reintroduction of paganism through the New Age movement, somehow they feel that they are immune. Few would believe that such blatant acts of rebellion could ever happen to them or that a counterfeit Christianity could ever occur in the denominations where they worship. However, such is not the case. Year by year, there is a growing trend in Christianity, showing that Christians are embracing various teachings that literally deify man and tap into metaphysical techniques used in the occult.

The Last Time Around

If history does repeat itself, and as Solomon said, there is "nothing new under the sun," is it possible that history may repeat itself for the last time? If the signs of the times indicate that

we are living at a time when Jesus could
return, should Christians be aware of the
possibility that this time of deception could
affect them as well? The doctrines of demons,
that Paul talked about with Timothy, would be
directed at believers. The apostasy that Paul
warned about refers to believers falling away
from faith in the Word of God and sound
doctrine based upon the Scriptures. For our
generation to disregard this warning, is not
only wrong, it is part of the great delusion of the
last days.

Accountable to Whom?

There are many Christian leaders like
Rodney Howard–Browne, John Wimber and
Paul Cain who have endorsed this "new
spirituality" and believe it is a move of God.
However, numerous well–respected leaders do
not. The teachers of the "new spirituality"
claim that they could not possibly be outside of
the will of God because they have tested the
spirits. They say that they are accountable to
other Christians who support their actions and
beliefs.

Of course, everyone needs to be accountable.
It is just as important that the ones we are
accountable to, are also accountable to the Word
of God. If those we are accountable to are not
basing their wisdom and discernment on
Scripture, then the door has been opened for all
kinds of heresy in the name of Christ.

Influences From the East

The prophets of the Old Testament pleaded
with their people to turn back to God. Jeremiah
was deeply distressed over what was happening

as the people were moving further and further away from God. He warned:

> A conspiracy has been found among the men of Judah and among the inhabitants of Jerusalem. They have turned back to the iniquities of their ancestors who refused to hear My words, and they have gone after other gods to serve them; the house of Israel and the house of Judah have broken My covenant which I have made with their fathers, Therefore, thus says the Lord, Behold, I am bringing disaster on them which they will not be able to escape.[115]

Isaiah appealed to the people of his generation who had strayed far from God:

> Come house of Jacob and let us walk in the light of the Lord. For thou hast abandoned Thy people, the house of Jacob, because they are filled with influences from the East, and they are soothsayers like the Philistines and they strike bargains with the children of foreigners.[116]

Are the words of the prophets valid for us today when it comes to distancing ourselves from spiritual deception? Let us take heed to the warnings of both the Old Testament and New Testament writers who were inspired by God to warn our generation of the potential downfalls that lead God's people astray.

Time Will Tell

Certainly, time will determine whether or not those who are cautious about the "new spirituality" are right or wrong. If it is

---

[115] Jeremiah 11:9-11.

[116] Isaiah 2:5-6.

genuinely from the Holy Spirit, then the fruit we see produced in the future will be obvious: a desire for repentance and holy living; a zeal to witness and share the gospel; a burden for the poor and the needy; a zeal to glorify the Lord Jesus Christ and His Word. However, if we continue to see biblical revelation being superseded by human experience, the future looks grim.

Hold Fast to the Word

Paul's words to Titus for the church at Crete provide excellent advice for all believers today. He told them to be

hospitable, loving what is good, sensible, just, devout, self-controlled, holding fast to the faithful word which is in accordance with the teaching, that (you) may be able to exhort in sound doctrine to refute those who contradict.[117]

Paul taught that sensible, devout, self-controlled believers hold fast to God's Word. Should this be the goal of every Bible-believing Christian?

---

[117] Titus 1:8-9.

Chapter XII
Back to Basics

Most Christians believe that we are living in the most important time this world has ever known, and that the return of Jesus Christ is at hand. If this is true, then what should be our focus? Has God called us into the family of God for such a time as this? Should we make every possible effort to dedicate our lives to Him by doing everything possible to reach out to the lost with the good news that the Gospel transforms people out of darkness into the Kingdom of God? What efforts are we making to accomplish this purpose?

In writing to the Corinthians, the apostle Paul talked about the excellence of love. As we read his words, it should help us to get our priorities right. He said:

If I speak with the tongues of men and of angels, but do not have love, I have become a noisy gong or a clanging cymbal. And if I have the gift of prophecy and know all the mysteries and all knowledge; and if I have all faith, so as to remove mountains, but do not have love, I am nothing. And if I

*give all my possessions to the poor, and if I
deliver my body to be burned, but do not
have love, it profits me nothing. Love is
patient, love is kind, and is not jealous, love
does not brag and is not arrogant, does not
act unbecomingly; it does not seek its own, is
not provoked, does not take into account a
wrong suffered, does not rejoice in
unrighteousness, but rejoices with the
truth...*[118]

How refreshing these words are at a time
when we see the body of Christ polarizing and
headed in separate ways! Why is it that at a
time in our earth's history when there is so
much strife, so many people are seeking self–
empowerment, self–gratification and self–
gain? It would be great if everyone of us could
take Paul's words and apply them to our
everyday lives.

When Jesus was asked by a Pharisee
lawyer which was the greatest commandment
of the Law, He responded by quoting
Deuteronomy 6:5: "'You shall love the Lord your
God with all you heart, and with all your soul
and with all your mind,' this is the great and
foremost commandment." Then, He
immediately quoted Leviticus 19:18: "And a
second is like it, 'You shall love your neighbor
as yourself.' On these two commandments
depend the whole Law and the Prophets."[119]

Jesus summarized the whole Old Testament
with these two verses. It is interesting that both
of these verses talk about love – God's love for

---

118   1 Corinthians 13:1-6.
119   Matthew 23:34-40.

us, and the fact that once we have received this love, we are instructed to give His love away to others.

This is what Christianity is all about! How is it that we as Christians can get so far out of focus and begin to go astray because we have left our supreme calling which comes from the very heart of God? Next time you feel that Christianity is getting too dull or that you're tired of the status quo, or that your church is too dead and you thought God had packed up and moved away– STOP and think for a moment about God's love, as He hung there on the cross for you. When we recognize the kind of love Jesus Christ expressed for us, all our selfish trivial pursuits will fall into their proper place, and truly we will be more "on fire" for God.

Jesus Said It

Throughout the time that Jesus ministered here on earth there were always those who opposed what He was teaching or would try to trick Him with questions that would trap Him according to the Law. Although these individuals shaped their questions and statements in order to advance their own personal agendas, Jesus always answered them with wisdom and truth.

On one occasion the Pharisees approached Him and asked the question: "Is it lawful to give a poll tax to Caesar or not?" Jesus perceived their malice and said: "Why are you testing Me, you hypocrites?" Then after taking from them a denarius, one of the Roman coins used for the poll tax, He showed them Caesar's inscription on one side. He then replied to their question: "Then render to Caesar the things that are Caesar's and to God the things that are God's."[120]

On the same day, some Sadducees came to Him, and tried to ask a trick question that would stump Jesus and advance their view that there was no resurrection for the dead. He answered their question, but before He did He proclaimed the following words: "You are mistaken, not understanding the **Scriptures,** or the **power** of God."[121]

It is with this verse in mind, that I have written this book. An effective Christian is one that recognizes that the Word of God and the power of God should always be balanced. It is not the Word of God alone nor is it the power of God's Holy Spirit alone. It is a balance between the two.

Let us continue in the battle for lost souls. May we be open and willing to be led as the Holy Spirit works in our lives, while at the same time remembering the Word of God is our absolute guide.

The Last Word

The apostle Peter, as he was concluding his second letter as recorded in the Bible, was writing at a time in history when the Gnostic heresies were infecting the church in a very powerful way. Gnosticism was a brand of Christian mysticism, not unlike many of the popular teachings that are floating around the church today. Peter exhorted the reader with the assurance that Christ's coming is a future

---

120   Matthew 22:15-22.
121   Matthew 22:23-33.

reality that will both destroy the world and bring a new heavens and a new earth.

When we read his words today it helps us to get our focus on what is important, as well as to help us understand why genuine believers can go astray. Peter wrote:

> *Since all these things are to be destroyed in this way, what sort of people ought you to be in holy conduct and godliness, looking for and hastening the coming day of God, on account of the heavens will be destroyed by burning, and the elements will melt with intense heat! But according to His promise we are looking for new heavens and a new earth, in which righteousness dwells. Therefore, beloved, since you look for these things, be diligent to be found by Him in peace, spotless and blameless, and regard the patience of our Lord to be salvation; just as our beloved Paul, according to the wisdom given him, wrote to you, as also in all his letters, speaking in them of these things, in which are some things hard to understand, which the untaught and unstable distort, as they do also the rest of the Scriptures, to their own destruction.* [122]

Regarding the subject of shallow–rooted Christianity and the apostasy that it produces, we should further investigate Paul's warnings relating to this matter. As Paul wrote:

> *In pointing these things out to the brethren, you will be a good servant of Jesus Christ, constantly nourished on the words of the faith and of the sound doctrine which you have been following. But have nothing to do with worldly fables fit only for old women. On*

---

[122] 2 Peter 3:11-16.

the other hand discipline yourself for the purpose of godliness.[123]

And then the words of Paul, which I believe provide the solution to the difficulty Christianity is facing today. If all of us would act upon these words, I am certain our differences could be resolved and we would go on and serve God and honor His name:

I solemnly charge you in the presence of God and in Christ Jesus, who is to judge the living and the dead, and by His appearing and His kingdom: preach the word; be ready in season and out of season; reprove, rebuke, exhort, and with great patience and instruction. For the time will come when they will not endure sound doctrine, but wanting to have their ears tickled, they will accumulate teachers in accordance with their own desires; and will turn their ears away from the truth, and will turn aside to myths. But you be watchful in all things, endure hardship, do the work of an evangelist, fulfill your ministry.[124]

The real focus and meaning of Christianity is that all believers should be involved in evangelism in some way. We are to be witnesses of the faith to a needy world around us. Jesus placed a high priority on witnessing, for it was the last subject He talked about before He ascended into Heaven. He stated:

You shall receive power when the Holy Spirit has come upon you; and you shall be My witnesses both in Jerusalem, and in all Judea

---

[123] 1 Timothy 4:6-7.

[124] 2 Timothy 4:1-5.

*and Samaria, and even to the remotest part
of the earth.* [125]

The power of the Holy Spirit has been given
to man for the purpose of enhancing our
witnessing abilities which in every case should
bring glory and honor to Jesus Christ. Let us
distance ourselves from the kind of self-
serving "what's in it for me" kind of
Christianity and forget about ourselves and
serve others. Let us do all that we can to put our
focus back on Jesus Christ and His Word. Then
and only then will we have accomplished the
perfect will of the Father.

---

[125] Acts 1:8.

Epilogue

Recently, I was observing sea gulls feeding along a beach near Sydney, Australia, when God spoke to me in a powerful way. The gulls had flocked there because they knew that they were going to be fed. People were throwing pieces of food from their picnic lunches to them. Although most were throwing chunks of bread and meat, I noticed one person fooling them by tossing chunks of a Styrofoam cup which the gulls were gobbling up as if it were food.

Almost instantaneously, I saw an analogy. Christians, like gulls, seek to be fed – gulls physically to grow naturally, Christians spiritually so that they can draw closer to God. And as with the Styrofoam that the gulls were eating, some Christians consume spiritual food in the name of Christianity that is not Christian at all.

Although the gulls thought they were eating food, the Styrofoam provided no nutritional value. In fact, if the gulls continued to eat this material as a steady diet, they would eventually die.

May God give each one of us a desire to feast upon the bread of life – His Word – so that we can be assured of a well–balanced diet and live our lives effectively for Him.

Appendix

On December 5, 1995, John Wimber and several directors of the Association of Vineyard Churches traveled to Toronto, Canada to announce an important decision they had made. For almost two years, the Toronto Airport Vineyard had become the "Mecca" for an experience called the "Toronto Blessing" which had been spreading all over the world. Wimber and his colleagues made this trip to announce that the Toronto Airport Vineyard was to be disengaged from the Association of Vineyard Churches.

Supporters and even critics of the "Toronto Blessing" were shocked when the announcement came. When the news hit the Internet after the December 5th meeting, nearly everyone was confused regarding what the separation meant. John Wimber had just endorsed John Arnott's new book called the *Father's Blessing* by saying he believed that the senior pastor of the Airport Vineyard Church had experienced an authentic visitation from God.[126] So what could have happened to cause John Wimber to change his mind?

As with every dispute and division that occurs in the church, there are always two sides. John Arnott, writing in the first edition of *Spread the Fire*, February 1996, explained his

---

[126] John Arnott, *The Father's Blessing* (Creation House, Strang Communications Co.), back cover endorsement.

perspective of why the division occurred by saying: "The bottom line, we were told, is that the [Association of Vineyard Churches] board felt Toronto Airport Vineyard renewal services were not mirroring the Vineyard model. Rather than ask us to revamp the renewal meetings, they released us to continue as we believe God is leading us."[127]

Although John Arnott's communication in the *Spread the Fire* newsletter makes it sound like the Toronto disassociation was congenial and without any major differences, a report sent out by regional director Happy Leman to inform Vineyard pastors about the expulsion seems to reflect another perspective. In a two page letter that appeared on the Internet dated December 8, 1995, Leman stated: "The Association of Vineyard Churches and the Toronto Airport Vineyard seem to have fundamental differences in philosophy regarding the pastoral administration of this Renewal."[128]

Further, Leman pointed out other reservations that the Association of Vineyard Churches had regarding the so-called renewal in Toronto. Some of these concerns included people being "hyped" or manipulated, an "emerging prophetic theology" that promoted an

---

127 John Arnott, "Here's Where We Stand," *Spread the Fire* (February, 1996), 6.

128 sender new wine@grmi.org., December 13, 1995- Letter send to Vineyard pastors in the Midwest Region by Happy Leman, Regional Overseer, Association of Vineyard Churches, December 8, 1995.

end times "elitist mentality," abuses in behavior including "demonic activity," and the encouragement or spotlighting of "extra-biblical manifestations."[129]

On January 20, 1996, the Toronto Airport Vineyard was renamed the Toronto Airport Christian Fellowship.[130] Although the name of the church in Toronto has changed, the "Toronto Blessing" still continues to spread around the world and shows no signs of slowing down.

---

[129] Ibid.

[130] Krysia Lear and Daina Doucet, *Spread the Fire*, "From Division to Multiplication" (February, 1996), 4.

About the Author

Roger Oakland is an author–lecturer who speaks internationally on a variety of subjects relating to how the Bible helps us understand the past, what is happening in the world today and where we are headed in the future.

A catalog of other books and audio–visual materials that he has developed which strengthen the faith of Christians and challenge unbelievers about what they believe, can be obtained by contacting his ministry offices in the following locations:

Understand The Times
P.O. Box 27239
Santa Ana, CA U.S.A. 92799

Understand The Times
P.O. Box 1160
Eston, Saskatchewan, Canada SOL 1AO

Understand The Times
Hall Street, New Stevenston
Motherwell, Scotland U.K. ML 4LX

or call... 1 (800) 689–1888